COMMENTS

"These stories of hope for women facing unplanned pregnancies and their unborn children will touch your heart with the truth that there is a plan for everyone's life, and there is One who is watching and bringing that plan to completion."

Kurt Entsminger
President of Care Net

"Good for you, Jeanetta. I commend you on your book. Having one child, another one on the way and a husband who was adopted, I have a new understanding of what a blessing the birth of a child can be. If my husband's birth mother had not made the difficult choice of giving him up for adoption thirty-two years ago, I would never have met such a wonderful man who has given me two of the best gifts in the world, my children. I am thankful for her strength each and every day. I hope your book is not only a tremendous success, but is an inspiration to us all!"

Erika H. Westmoreland
Vice President, Marketing
THE WALK THE TALK Company
Proud mother of 16 month old and baby due January 2006

"Despite a virtual media blackout, pregnancy care centers across America are providing a much needed service helping unwed mothers and their babies. This new book powerfully tells the stories of some of them."

All the best,
Jerry Newcombe
Senior Producer
Coral Ridge Ministries - TV

"WOW! What a wonderful book Jeanetta Pollard has written. In this day and time, with morals slipping every day, it is refreshing to see that while there are consequences to our bad decisions, there are decision to be made all along the way, and that you <u>can</u> have the best possible outcome. I've heard it said that we are not our mistakes, we are our possibilities. I have several relatives who have been touched by unplanned pregnancies, and I will be sending each of them a copy of this fabulous book."

Well done, Jeanetta.
Julie Boyd
Franklin, Tennessee

"I just read several of the chapter selections from your new book and was touched and impressed with your stories. Your pro-life advocacy is supported by the stories you share. Many of the stories are up-lifting and have a happy ending, while others take the reader down the path of sadness and the reality of abortion outcomes.

I have been touched by your stories, particularly "Tiny Tim." Please keep this book in the hands of those who will be challenged with this life changing decision."

Barbara Fielder
Author - *I'm Communicating, but...am I Being Heard?;*
Motivation in the Workplace; and *Missy the Kitty* children's books.

"The old saying says that, if you want to see the rainbow, you have to put up with the rain. This inspiring and uplifting new work by Jeanetta Pollard will prove to be quite a rainbow for some of those who have just come in from the rain. This is a fantastic read that will bring hope to the hopeless and touch the untouchable. Pollard never ceases to amaze!"

Austin Madding
Teenage Comic Book Author and Illustrator

"This book is truly stories of hope. While each story is heart wrenching, what an awesome testament to God's grace and love. Every child conceived is never a mistake, but a God planned life. It was so exciting to hear how God was at work in the lives of the people involved in each story. I thank God for the people He has placed in the paths of these young ladies and these precious children."

Rita Templeton

"Unwanted pregnancy can generate feelings of conflict, anger, depression, and hopelessness. Politically correct action and council of Planned Parenthood advises a person to have an abortion. Jeanetta's book provides a positive solution of Mercy and Grace through real stories of others who have faced pregnancy. *Stories of Hope* is an excellent resource to provide a person or organization that counsels girls who are pregnant."

Bill George
Church Planting Strategist
Tennessee Baptist Convention

"I have read all the stories in the sampling of your book and found all to be very touching, especially about *Tiny Tim*.

This book should be mandatory reading for anyone considering abortion."

Rosemary Browning
Symsonia, Kentucky

Stories of
HOPE
A Book About Choices

Compiled and Edited by

JEANETTA BEARDEN POLLARD

Success Ranch Publishers
P.O. Box 7
Boaz, Kentucky 42027-0007

ISBN 978-0-9722377-2-7
Library of Congress 2005906757

Cover Design by Dan Sheppard and Nancy McDonald
Three Baby Photographs on Cover (Sunflower Baby, Pink Boa Baby and 'From
God' with Bow Baby) © Maria Hurty
Photograph of Editor by Katrina Awbery

All book correspondence should be addressed to:
Jeanetta Bearden Pollard
P.O. Box 7
Boaz, Kentucky 42027-0007

Success Ranch Publishers
P.O. Box 7
Boaz, Kentucky 42027-0007

DEDICATION

This book is dedicated to all those who work in pregnancy care centers. Many of these dedicated workers are volunteers. They ask no other reward than to serve those whose lives they touch.

And to all those others who support the centers financially, without your contributions, this work could not go on.

May God continue to bless each of you as you continue to minister to women and men in their unplanned pregnancies, and to open the eyes of the world to the fact that this is a baby, not a blob of tissue.

"Blessed is he who has regard for the weak;
The Lord delivers him in times of trouble.
The Lord will protect him and preserve his life;
He will be blessed in the land and not
Surrender him to the desire of his foes.
The Lord will sustain him on his sickbed
And restore him from his bed of illness.

Psalms 41:1-3 NIV

CONTENTS

Acknowledgments 13

Introduction 15

1. ADOPTION

Sacrificial Love 20

The Rest of the Story 30

A Magnificent, Miraculous Happening 33

I Don't Know Who the Father Is 39

Heroes 41

An Open Adoption 43

Stacy's Story 47

2. SAVED FROM ABORTION

If I'm Pregnant, I Must Have an Abortion 54

His Love Reaching 57

No Easy Choices..60

Too Far Along to Have an Abortion 63

I Have to Kill My Baby 65

Never Alone...67

Freedom That Guarantees Peace 70

I Don't Trust Anybody...................................73

Two Lives Saved 75

The Sanctity of Human Life 77
Thank You...80
Marriage Just Doesn't Work 82
The Life Chain 84
Laurie 85
Do You Remember Me? 87
I Have Been So Blessed 91
A Letter to Glenda 94
Thank You for Telling the Truth 97

3. ABSTINENCE

Hope For Tomorrow 100
Wrong Choices Cause Painful Consequences 102
The Gift of The Second Chance 104
Negative Test Can Have Positive Influence 106
If Only..109
The Whole Truth..113
Purity Regained 115

4. ABORTION

To Be or Not To Be.....................................120
The Story of Tiny Tim 121
What About His Freedom To Choose.....................126
He Turned His Face Toward Me.........................128

Sometimes You Just Need
    to Get Another Perspective 135
Abortion Breaks the Heart of God 137

5. STORIES OF HOPE

I Had No Idea 142
The Friendship Factor 145
Don't Worry Babe, I'll Take Care of Everything 149
A Day in the Life of A Pregnancy Center................151
Men of Hope..153
Divine Appointment 155
Time Changes Things..157
Hope..158
I Want to Grow Up 161
It's No Accident That I'm Here 164
A Different Kind of Prayer 166

6. YOUR CHILD MAY BE MENTALLY OR PHYSICALLY CHALLENGED

Arms Filled With Babies... 170
We Give Thanks.. 175
Mother's Day 177
Double the Love.. 179
Baby Samuel's Story.. 183

7. POST ABORTION

Sisters In Christ 188
Melody Rose...189
One Woman's Story...194
Post Abortion Healing 196
This Far the Lord Has Brought Me 198

Parental Notification..203
A Message to Those Fighting the Pro-Life Battle...207
Where to Find Help 211

ACKNOWLEDGMENTS

Most books would not be written without the help and encouragement of many wonderful people. *Stories of Hope* is no exception.

I am grateful to my husband, Jim, and to the rest of our family who are always there to help and encourage me as I struggle with "this and that." Without Jim, this book would not be possible. He is always there to assist me.

My special thanks goes to Nancy McDonald, my long-time friend and the Executive Director of Hope Pregnancy Centers of Broward County, Florida. Nancy caught my vision as soon as I sent my book proposal to her. It is she who has done so much of the work for this book. She wrote stories; she cajoled others into submitting their stories, and then she edited or rewrote these stories.

It was, indeed, Nancy who several years ago asked me to serve on the Board of Directors for Hope Pregnancy Centers. This is where my true passion for the lives of the unborn and their mothers and fathers was birthed.

The Board of Directors of Hope caught this vision from Nancy and became as excited about is as Nancy and I were. Our dear friend, Robin Lewis, chairman of the Board of Directors of HPC, was a true supporter and "cheerleader." Thanks to all of you board members, who for the most part, knew nothing about me other than what Nancy and Robin told you, and yet you believed in me and this project.

I am grateful to my dear friend, Rena Faye Boyd, who has again, even in the midst of moving, taken the time to proofread this manuscript. Her knowledge of English and proper use of grammar is indispensable. To this list of those I appreciate so much also are my friends, Peggy Watkins, who also proofread the book and to Dan Sheppard for ALL of his assistance. He helped solve a lot of problems!

To those who have contributed stories or who have given permission for their stories to be told in this book, goes my heartfelt thanks. I thank you so much because telling these stories can make you vulnerable; it can bring back painful memories - memories you would rather stay buried forever. You have been willing to bare your souls - to tell of mistakes you have made in the hope that people who read this book *can learn that there is hope no matter what your life has been like in the past.*

Thanks to the staff and volunteers of Hope for Life for reviewing the stories. Hope for Life was the second center where I was privileged to serve on the Board of Directors.

And, finally, I am appreciative to God who is the One who can change lives by giving people hope and by continually telling them, *"There is a purpose and a plan for each and every one of you."*

INTRODUCTION

Several years ago I was asked to serve on the Board of Directors of Hope Pregnancy Centers in Broward County, Florida. I had been pro-life ever since I could remember, but when I served on the Board, my real education about this issue began. When I learned that each year there were more abortions in Miami-Dade County than there were live births, it broke my heart. Broward County, just to the north, was the number two county in Florida for abortions. How could this be?

Many of you have probably seen the question posed somewhere: "Why hasn't God sent someone with a cure for AIDS or cancer?" Perhaps God's answer might be: "I did send someone, but you aborted them." We don't know how many Einsteins, Abraham Lincolns, George Washingtons, Michangelos, Dwight Moodys, or other persons of inestimable value that God has sent to earth, but in our love affair with choice and convenience, we have aborted them.

The Bible tells us that God has a plan for each and every life. Have no doubt about it, from the moment the child is conceived everything about it is determined – the color of its eyes and hair, its sex, - virtually everything is present that will appear in the full-term child! All that has to happen is for time to pass and for growth to occur. God had a plan for that child even BEFORE it was created in its mother's womb. (Psalms 139:16)

With the invention of the Ultrasound Machine, the myth that the fetus is only a blob of tissue or a clump of cells has been exposed for the lie that it is. Women are able to see into the "window of the womb" and recognize that it is a child. Many pregnancy centers across the country are now offering free ultrasounds to clients to bring home the truth that it's a child – not a choice!

15

The battle for life is a battle that is fought in the spiritual realm. The warriors are those who serve as staff members and volunteers at pregnancy centers all over our nation. They fight the battle in the privacy of the counseling room, one life at a time. They see God at work in extraordinary ways.

I have heard the stories for years, and I have been overwhelmed with the idea that they must be told – told over and over again until people understand how precious every life is. That is why this book is being written. I want to tell the stories of hope…the hope and the future that God promises to every life. (Jeremiah 29:11)

This book tells a story of a woman who was raped yet carried the child and placed him for adoption, and he became an answer to one family's prayers for a child. It tells stories of many women and men who chose to carry their children to term when the truth was shared with them in the loving and safe environment of a pregnancy care center. The stories in this book tell of young people who are choosing abstinence until marriage in a society that promotes promiscuity. It tells the never-ending story of God's grace, His healing and reconciliation. It tells other stories of people whose lives have forever been changed for the better by a visit to a pregnancy care center.

The names in most of these stories have been changed to guard client confidentiality. The stories are all true and are used with permission.

This book has been done primarily in conjunction with Hope Pregnancy Centers, Inc. located in Broward County, Florida. It is a labor of love for the women and men who find themselves in unplanned pregnancies and for the unborn children they carry. It is my desire that your heart will be touched by these stories; and that you, too, might get involved in a pregnancy care center where you live and see the extravagant lengths that God goes to in order to protect the lives of these precious ones.

It has been said that all we need for evil to triumph is for

16

good people to do nothing. Abortion is an evil that has been present with us far too long. More than 50 million lives have been lost, just since the legalization of this practice in the United States in 1973. Weep for all that we have lost, but praise God that He is a forgiving and gracious Father who forgives us of ALL our sins when we ask. Even abortion.

ADOPTION

The first adoption recorded is found in Exodus 2:9-10: Pharaoh's daughter said to her, "Take this baby and nurse him for me, and I will pay you." So the woman took the baby and nursed him. When the child grew older, she took him to Pharaoh's daughter and he became her son. She named him Moses...

SACRIFICIAL LOVE

1 Kings 3:16-28

Now two prostitutes came to the king and stood before him. One of them said, "My lord, this woman and I live in the same house. I had a baby while she was there with me. The third day after my child was born, this woman also had a baby. We were alone; there was no one in the house but the two of us.

During the night this woman's son died because she lay on him. So she got up in the middle of the night and took my son from my side while I your servant was asleep. She put him by her breast and put her dead son by my breast. The next morning, I got up to nurse my son-and he was dead! But when I looked at him closely in the morning light, I saw that it wasn't the son I had borne."

The other woman said, "No! The living one is my son; the dead one is yours." But the first one insisted, "No! The dead one is yours; the living one is mine." And so they argued before the king.

The king said, "This one says, 'My son is alive and your son is dead,' while that one says, 'No! Your son is dead and mine is alive.'" Then the king said, "Bring me a sword." So they brought a sword for the king. He then gave an order: "Cut the living child in two and give half to one and half to the other."

The woman whose son was alive was filled with compassion for her son and said to the king, "Please, my lord, give her the living baby! Don't kill him!" But the other said, "Neither I nor you shall have him. Cut him in two!"

Then the king gave his ruling: "Give the living baby to the first woman. Do not kill him; she is his mother." ~ 1 Kings 3:16-28 NIV

Adoption is a subject that is sure to evoke an emotional response. While our society (especially in Christian circles) is quick to rejoice when Mr. and Mrs. Childless Couple adopt a baby, they don't know quite what to say to the pregnant woman who announces that she is placing her child for adoption. Whether it is spoken or not, the question that hangs in the air is, "How could you give your baby away?"

We hear it all the time in the counseling room at the pregnancy care centers. The client comes in, and she is planning on having an abortion, if her pregnancy test is positive. We share the truth with her and talk to her about her options. One of the options we always want to talk about is adoption.

The most frequent answer we hear is this: "I could never give my baby away." A logical thinker immediately identifies that the two thoughts are diametrically opposed to each other. You are planning to terminate the life of the child that you love so much you can't 'give it away'??? Ludicrous? Yes. Tragic? Most certainly. But this unreasonable response is all too common in our self-centered society.

The story from I Kings that opens this account exemplifies the kind of sacrificial love that is required for placing a child for adoption. The birth mother who stood before King Solomon was willing to give up her rights to her child so that he would have an opportunity for life. Birth mothers who have this kind of courage are heroes and should be revered in our society.

Throughout history mothers have sacrificed much for the sake of their children. The mother who chooses to place her child in the hands of people who can care for it and love it and provide a family is making the greatest sacrifice of all.

There is such a mother somewhere in this world that I will be eternally grateful for. I have never met her or talked with her, but I thank God every day that she was honest enough with herself to know that she was not prepared to raise a child. I thank God that she wanted something better for her child than she could provide. **I am an adoptive parent, and this is my story of how God brought children to our home.**

21

We married young and had such beautiful dreams for our future – for the goals we would accomplish and for the family we would raise. There would be a little girl who would look just like her daddy and wrap him around her little finger. There would be a little boy who would look just like his mommy and grow up to be someone important. But there was a carefully timed schedule, too. There were careers to build, homes to buy, and educations to complete. The fear of pregnancy at the "wrong" time was the constant daily reminder to be careful and use birth control faithfully. The years flew by, and the "right" time came; we were ready for the Parenthood Phase of The Plan For Our Life.

We were still ready the next year, and the next. We made the rounds, visiting specialists and fertility clinics. I took fertility drugs, and had tests and various 'procedures', and on our ninth wedding anniversary we were told that we would probably never conceive a child of our own.

We decided it was time to move on with our lives. The Things To Do list included Travel, so we took our savings, bought new luggage and went to Europe. The excitement of planning the trip helped take away the dull ache of knowing we might remain childless. We promised our friends a big party to share pictures when we returned. The trip was wonderful; the photographs were better than we could have imagined, and the dinner party was on for Friday night.

I spent most of the day in bed, knowing that I was coming down with the flu. I was just so tired. I slept late in the morning, napped in the afternoon, and was ready for bed by nine PM. Yes…you guessed it. I was pregnant. Wonder of wonder, miracle of miracles. Like Hannah[1], God had granted us the petition that we had asked of Him. Our son was born nine months after our European vacation! After a year or so, we began to pray that God

---

[1] Read Hannah's story in I Samuel chapter 1

would send us another child. That little girl was still a dream that we held dear.

One year – two years – three years. No baby. Quadruple doses of fertility drugs. At some point in time you start to ask God, "Is this what you want us to do, or is there another way?"

We began to explore the possibility of adoption, and connected with a local Christian agency. We were approved and our baby was due on our fourteenth wedding anniversary. We waited with baited breath for the phone call. The call came, but it was not the news we had been waiting for. "The birth mother has decided to parent the baby. We're very sorry, but you knew all along that this was possible."

Yes, we knew – but we never believed that it could happen to us. "Was it a boy or a girl?" was the only response I could come up with. A healthy baby girl, but don't worry, we will just put your name back in the pool and our next baby will be yours." Disappointment and anger warred for first place in my emotional responses. Somewhere deep down I did trust God, but my human reaction was overriding my trust. Wasn't that OUR baby girl, God?

Of course our son, now four-years-old, had questions of his own. Being a lawyer's son, he thought we should probably sue someone! In explaining to him that God's ways are not our ways, I began to experience peace in my own heart. I really did believe that God was in control.

Two weeks later, I received a phone call from one of my best friends. She and her husband were friends with a young pastor and his wife who lived in a nearby town, and they had gone to visit them just days before.

They were surprised to learn that the pastor and his wife were caring for a little girl who was the granddaughter of a lady in their congregation. The teen mom was really struggling and was considering the possibility of placing the baby for adoption. The pastor and his wife were the natural choice; they had two little boys, had been told they couldn't have more children, and desperately wanted a little girl. It seemed like the perfect answer for everyone involved.

It just wasn't God's plan. In casual conversation, my friends asked this sweet couple to pray for us – their friends that were involved in an adoption which fell through. They drove home and never gave the conversation another thought.

But the pastor and his wife gave the conversation much more thought. They couldn't sleep that night. They stood over the crib where this precious baby slept and prayed for God to show them what to do. They were already in love with her. They already thought of her as their child, even though the legalities were not initiated. They talked about what it would be like to accept the fact that their family was complete without a daughter.

Over the next two weeks, they talked to the birth mother, to the grandmother, and reached their decision. This was not their baby; it was ours. They made the phone call that morning and just a few hours later, my daughter was in my arms. The consent forms were signed by both the birth mother and father in the next forty-eight hours, and we had miraculously become parents again!

Isaiah 60:22b says, "I am the LORD; in its time I will do this swiftly." Wow! He certainly was. We had so many opportunities to tell people how God had worked in our life. We were filled with great joy because we believed we had seen His hand at work. One of the precious confirmations that we saw happen was the day we went to pick up the baby.

Before they brought her out to meet us, the pastor and his wife just shared some things with me about her life up to that point. She was almost six months old, but because of the lack of attention, was not very responsive to outside stimuli. In their words, "She just kind of lives in her own little world. She doesn't cry a lot, but she also has never smiled. She doesn't like to be held – most of her time before she came to us was spent in an infant seat. The pediatrician says all that will change in time, but don't expect too much too fast." My heart rose to the challenge, but I cautioned myself to take it easy.

Before we left our house that afternoon to go and meet the baby, I let my 4-year-old look through the baby toys we had purchased just weeks before. "Would you like to take a toy to your new baby sister?" I asked him. He chose a huge, brightly colored rattle, and we were off.

We sat in the tiny living room of the pastor's house and held out our arms to receive this child that the Lord was delivering into our hands. She came to me without hesitation, but with a somber face.

My little boy approached her tentatively and held the rattle out to her. Her precious face lit up with the biggest smile in the world – it was like God's rainbow of promise was all over that little living room! Every adult in the room was in tears – God's goodness was so evident and His Spirit was so present! The pastor and his wife both said later that if there had been any lingering doubts, God erased them all with that smile!

We had our miracle son when the doctors said we would never conceive. We had our daughter who was provided by His gracious and generous plan. We had just built a new home that was designed with the faith that there would be a second child someday. God had allowed us to achieve most every dream that we had put on that list so many years before. As I look back, I realize that we were almost smug in our satisfaction with the place where we had arrived.

This would be a perfect place to end our adoption story and refer you back to the passage in I Kings about the sacrificial love of birth mothers. I was certainly thankful for the heroic birth mother who had recognized her limitations and loved her little girl enough to place her in the arms of a loving family who could provide for her and protect her. I was so glad that she had chosen life for this child and not abortion. But the story didn't end there.

Almost six months to the day that we became parents of

this beautiful little girl, someone knocked on my door. I was so surprised to see the pastor's wife standing there. Of course, as an adoptive parent who had seen all the TV movies, I always think, "what if she ever tries to get the baby back?" When I saw this woman's tear-streaked face, I feared the worst. She came in and sat down and told me an amazing story.

"Do you know anyone who might want to adopt a little boy? We really didn't know this information six months ago, but apparently your daughter's birth mother was already pregnant again when she signed the consent forms for the little girl. Maybe she didn't even know that she was pregnant again. She delivered prematurely almost two months ago. They didn't think the baby would live, but he has proven to be quite a fighter. He was in the hospital neo-natal unit for six weeks. She has been living in a car with him for the last two weeks and now he is very sick. She is ready to give him up – she knows she can't take care of him. Do you know anyone who might want him?"

Sometimes the obvious is very illusive. I referred her to the attorney who had handled the adoption for us. Days passed and my husband and I talked about other families we knew who might want to adopt.

In the meantime, the mother had signed consent forms and custody of the baby was temporarily placed with the attorney. A medical examination revealed that the baby had pneumonia, and he was put back in the hospital. (Months later the pediatrician said he didn't believe that the baby would live.)

We finally came up with the name of a couple who we knew were praying about adopting. My husband called them, explained the situation, and was met with silence on the other end of the phone. "Hello – are you there?" he asked, assuming that the good news had rendered the man speechless. Our friend cleared his throat and stumbled over his words, "Um – isn't that – I mean, I think that's YOUR baby." Silence again. Both ends of the line this time. They agreed to pray for God's wisdom.

My husband called me to relate the details of the conversation to me. I already knew. I had known the moment the pastor's wife told me the story. My husband knew. He knew the moment the attorney, our friend, called to say she had signed the consent. But our lives were perfect, and we weren't looking for anything that might change our little plan.

But God has gifts in store for us that we can't even dream or imagine. We talked, we prayed, and we spent a weekend thinking about it. We discussed it with our extended family. I went to my mother's house for the weekend and talked with her, with my grandmother, and with my favorite aunt.

No one thought this was a good idea. People said things to us like, "That's just what you need...another baby. You've got your hands full with these two kids...why do you need another one?"

I left there on Sunday afternoon feeling drained and more confused than ever. To make matters worse, my daughter screamed for most of the three hour trip home, and my four-year-old son joined in when the frustration of not being able to make her stop crying set in. I drove down the turnpike in tears myself, knowing what God was telling me to do and wondering if I were able to do it.

As I thought about all the arguments for and against adopting another child, I realized that all of my reasons for saying no were the same reasons that people use to justify abortion. God allows a life to be formed and women decide daily to snuff out that life because it isn't convenient.

This teenager had given a precious gift to the world in that baby boy – having already faced the pain of placing one baby for adoption, she could so easily have chosen to abort this little boy.

God had spoken clearly to me. He had put the same knowledge in my husband's heart, so we took lots of deep breaths and took the parental plunge one last time.

We brought him home from the hospital on a Monday. It

was the day he was actually due to be born and he was already two months old, even though he only weighed seven pounds. He and his sister have birthdays that are just ten months apart, and our life was a little crazy for a few years…making the adjustment from ten years of childlessness to a crew of three!

I like to explain it to people this way: Our first son was a miracle and a testimony to the fact that God can prevail, even when the "experts" told us no; our daughter was a testimony to the fact that God wants to give us the desires of our hearts, and God knew we wanted that little girl – but this last baby – our unexpected son – is testimony to the fact that God just likes to give us gifts!

We have been blessed beyond measure by a teenager who loved her two babies with a sacrificial love. I pray for her every year on their birthdays, hoping that God has rewarded her for her sacrifice, that He has blessed her with other children, and that she is at peace with the decisions she made those many years ago to give these two babies a family.

~ a grateful mom
Hope Pregnancy Centers
Broward County, Florida

P.S.

Oh, yes – one more miracle…remember the struggling pastor and his wife who couldn't have any more children? Just about a year after we adopted our son, she became pregnant and gave birth to a little girl.

When the kids were teenagers, we had the opportunity to visit with them and hear their perspective of those few months – about the pain they experienced when God instructed them to give the baby to us, and how He had walked them from the valley of disappointment to the mountaintop of having their own little girl! God had blessed their ministry and had prospered them financially

28

as well.

They are serving today as leaders in a large church in another state. The home where we visited them was so beautiful – quite a far cry from the little place where they lived when they placed our daughter in our hands!

The fabric of our lives is forever entwined with other believers…I'm sure we will never know the fullness of it until we sit with Jesus in Heaven and have the holy discussions that begin, "Remember the time….?"

THE REST OF THE STORY

You would be surprised to know how many clients come to us, hear the truth and walk out the door – never to be seen by us again. As they leave, still confused and uncertain about the decisions that face them, all we can do is pray.

It is helpful for us to imagine each one of them as a little lamb, being held in the tight, protective grasp of a Heavenly Father who loves them and understands them far better than we ever could hope to. We pray and ask Him to show them the Way. We seldom get to hear the "rest of the story."

He sent one such lamb our way late in 2001. She knew that she was pregnant and she came, hoping that we would help her get an abortion. After being told that we did not provide abortions or referrals for abortion, she agreed to hear our counselor present information about abortion procedures and risks. She was shocked to hear how abortions were done. She told the counselor now that she knew the truth, she thought she would have a hard time having an abortion. When the counselor presented adoption as an

30

alternative, she seemed open to the idea, but noncommittal.

As she left the center, she gave us permission to call her and see how she was feeling. We sent her on her way with a bag of maternity clothes, a grocery store gift certificate and a booklet about adoption.

All of our attempts at follow-up failed. After several months, her file was closed. She became one of the lost lambs that we turn over to the Shepherd. Usually, we never know the end of the story, but we are totally at peace because we know that the Shepherd knows every sheep by name.

Some of our Centers open on Saturdays now. The abortion clinics are open seven days a week, so we have started offering Saturday hours at various locations, hoping to compete on some level. It is inconvenient, and most of our staff is unaccustomed to working weekends. **(Okay, I'll be honest – we even grumble about it a little bit.)** Then, days like this particular Saturday happen, and we stand before the Lord ashamed that we almost missed out on the incredible gift He wanted to give us. This is how it happened on one of those Saturdays…

She was about six months pregnant this time. She made an appointment to come in because she needed some baby items. When the new counselor asked her if she had ever been a client before, she said yes. As the story unfolded, we were so excited to realize that God had allowed us the privilege of seeing how He had rescued one lost lamb!

Although we felt frustrated when she left that day back in 2001, God had given her everything she needed to make a decision to choose life for her baby. I'm sure she wore out the pages of that little adoption book as she made a very courageous – and difficult – decision to place that baby for adoption.

Now, two years later, she is pregnant with a baby she will parent. She thanked the volunteer counselor over and over for "everything Hope has done for me."

Isn't that amazing? What we saw as a failure – as a "lost"

client, God was using for His glory! Of course, saving babies isn't the only business our Heavenly Father is in...He wants to save moms for all eternity, too. This time, when the counselor shared the Gospel, the lost lamb was found forever. She prayed to receive Christ and left our center last Saturday, a bag full of baby clothes in her hand and a song of praise in her heart.

It makes us re-think our attitudes about this Saturday thing...Pray for us as we hold out the Word of Life and entrust these lost lambs to the Shepherd who will do whatever it takes to save them. **We're looking forward to next Saturday!**

Hope Pregnancy Centers
Broward County, Florida

A MAGNIFICENT, MIRACULOUS HALPPENING

In our lives, God gives us choices to make and I made the wrong choice. Even in our choosing the wrong way, God still walks with us. Handel's Messiah says every valley in our life shall be exalted and every crooked path shall be made straight. God can make golden skies *even* when one walks through the storms.

My father was an alcoholic. He was physically abusive to my mother and my sister, but not to me. I would stand up to him and protect my mom and sister. But I loved my daddy. His gift of music was passed through to me.

I was sent to college by our Minister of Music to be groomed as a Minister of Music to work at the church. I went to college and graduated. A teacher suggested I go and audition at the Performing Arts Studio in Philadelphia to continue with my singing. I listened to that teacher's voice. Already crookedness was in my life. The theatrical company put me in musical comedy, and I loved it.

Some of my friends wanted to go to New York City to audition for a show. I drove them. At the auditions, they asked me if I weren't going to try out. I said, "No, I just drove." Then they ask me if I sang. I told them yes, and I tried out. I won the audition; so I went to New York. I was chosen for the *Music Man;* then *Wild Cat* with Martha Raye. We took *Wild Cat* on the road.

When we were on Long Island, my dance partner stepped on my foot and broke some of the bones in my foot. After the show that night, we were all invited to a cast party at the home of Betty Hutton's brother, Jimmy Donohue.

My foot was really hurting; therefore, I asked Martha Raye if they had something I could take for pain. My mother had always told me never to take medicine from anyone else and never to drink alcohol. This night I did both. I made some very bad choices.

When I awoke the next morning, I was lying on a strange bed in a strange house with my clothes on. I was very scared. I got up and ran out of the house. My car was the only car in the courtyard. I went to where my friends were staying, and I asked them why they had left me. They replied that the people at the party told them that I would be okay left alone.

I missed my period next month but didn't think much about it because I wasn't regular. After missing the next period, I was very concerned. I felt something had happened to me. I went to the doctor. She told me I was pregnant. I was shocked. This couldn't be happening to me. I had always been a "good" girl. Life stopped for me.

I told my best friend, Joan, that I had to have an abortion. She said she had no idea where to go, but she was sure my show business friends would know where I could go. They sent me to the Pocono Mountains. We went into the clinic. It was very dark. There was no one there. There were pictures of skeletons all over the walls. I felt like death was coming all over us.

At that time, I had no relationship with God, but I heard a voice that told me to leave this place. This is death, it seemed to say. Even as Samuel did not recognize the voice of God when He spoke to him, (I Samuel 3:4-9 *"Then the Lord called Samuel. Samuel answered, 'Here I am.' And he ran to Eli and said, 'Here I am; you called me.' But Eli said, 'I did not call; go back and lie down.' So he went and lay down. Again the Lord called, 'Samuel!' And Samuel got up and went to Eli and said, 'Here I am; you called me.' 'My son,' Eli said, 'I did not call; go back and lie down.' Now Samuel did not yet know the Lord: The word of the Lord had not yet been revealed to him…"*) I did not know at this time it was God who was speaking to me. I told Joan about the voice and she said, "Let's go."

On the way back to New Jersey, I decided I would carry the baby no matter what happened; I would go away so as not to bring any shame to my family. I would decide later what would happen to the baby and myself.

I went to Phoenix, Arizona where my mother's oldest sister was. She was living with another family, waiting for her apartment. I was packed in with this Catholic family who took me in and loved me. They kept telling me that I wasn't dirty and that I had a purpose. She just kept saying, "You've got a purpose."

A week before the baby was to be born, I wanted my mommy. I called her, told her all that had happened, and she came to me.

Because I was a rape victim, in the hospital I was isolated and put at the end of the hall. I gave birth to a baby boy. I was not allowed to see him or to touch him because they wanted me to make a decision about what I was going to do with him. That night when the nurses went on break, my mom and I sneaked down to the nursery and looked at him. He was beautiful. He had long fingers. I thought someday he will play a piano.

The adoption agency was there all the time. They felt it would be better if I let him be adopted, since I did not know who the father was.

I signed him over for adoption. The only thing I asked was that he be put into a loving Methodist denomination home and that they have the same educational status as I. They honored this.

I got myself together and went back home. I tucked that son down deep in my heart, and he stayed there for twenty-nine years.

I met a wonderful man. The night he asked me to marry him, I told him, "Dennis, there's a part of my life that I must share with you because some day it could be our future."

I told him about my son, Timothy. I had named him after my father although my father would not let me bring him home because at that time, an unwed mother, was a shameful thing. My father couldn't face the shame so he asked me not to bring him home. That's why I made the decision to give him up.

I told Dennis about Timothy. Dennis told me he could not hold that against me. He said, "If he ever comes into our lives, he will be my son, too."

We went on with our lives. Our lives had valleys and mountains. God is so great! At thirty-eight, thanks to my mother-in-law's prayers and God's grace, I became a Christian. I began to give God inch-by-inch that dark pocket in my life, my son, and inch-by-inch he healed it.

One Mother's Day while sitting in church, the Spirit of God came upon me and He told me, "Today it is okay to share Timothy with your daughters." They were twenty-two and twenty-three at the time and they did not know about Timothy.

A friend had told me that some day I was going to be really free, and I would be able to say I had three children. This was that day.

When I told the girls, I was so scared. I was afraid it would tarnish the image they had of me, but I trusted God. They just sobbed. My oldest daughter said, "All my life I have bugged you for a brother. Why didn't you share this with me?"

They got excited. They wanted to meet their brother, and they felt he had a right to meet us.

Dennis said, "We're all in this together. If this is what we want, we'll do it. But, we don't know who he is or where he is."

Shauna said, "Let's just trust God."

When I contacted the adoption agency I worked with, they said that in Arizona it is impossible to get records because it is a closed state. But the lady on the phone whispered, "I'll tell you how to do it and who to contact."

Within six months we had found Mark – his adopted name. He was twenty-nine years old, and he lived in Dallas, Texas.

I wrote the family a letter and told them how much I loved and appreciated them for what they had done for him; for giving him what I couldn't give to him. I told them I didn't want to burst into their home and take him away from them. I just wanted a little picture to see what he looked like.

Mark's mother called the adoption agency. She was very frightened. She wanted to know what I really wanted. She asked that we leave them alone. I honored that for a year. During this time, I continued to walk with God.

The verse of scripture God gave me was Psalm 23.

After a year, the girls encouraged me to write him a letter. They each wrote their own letters and I mailed them.

The following Monday night, the phone rang. Dennis answered. I saw his eyes get red with tears. He said, "Karin, you need to talk to this person."

I picked up the phone and this voice said, *"Hello, Mom, this is Mark, your son. I've wanted to talk to you all my life."* We talked for about three hours.

Three days later, our whole family flew to San Antonio, where we met Mark.

Later he wrote me a letter. *It started, "Dear Brand New, Lovely Mother."* He thanked me for loving him when he was in my womb. You could have easily aborted me if you wanted to but you chose to give me life and I am so thankful that you made that decision. He went on to tell me he had had and was still having a wonderful life. He told me his adoptive parents had raised him to be a respectful and very kind gentleman.

He spoke about how happy he was to have met all of us. He said the day he met us was one of the most exciting days of his life.

Some thirty years ago when I sat in that abortion clinic and God spoke to me (even before I knew Him) about the spirit of death that prevailed there, I had no idea that one day He would call me to be the Director of a Pregnancy Care Center. But He knew the plans He had for me. Truly I have seen what my Catholic friend told me over and over - "You have a purpose" - even as we all do.

Karin Thomas, Executive Director
Hope Unlimited Family Care Center
Paducah, Kentucky

I DON'T KNOW WHO THE FATHER IS

It's hard to believe, but that statement is one that we hear frequently in the counseling room. Beautiful young women sit and stare at the positive pregnancy test on the table and count back the months on their fingers. If one man is the father, a positive test might be good news. If it is another man, abortion is the only solution they can see to the dilemma that their behavior has created.

We are living in a time of rampant immorality. It is on the television, in the movies and on signs and billboards everywhere we go. Many of our young people have been raised in a spiritual vacuum and don't even know the meaning of words like "abstinence" and "purity."

We see the havoc that this lifestyle brings into the lives of young women who never thought an unplanned pregnancy could happen to them. They tell us they were "careful"; they had "safe" sex...yet now they are pregnant and it feels like the end of the world to them!

"Leta" had other children and was in the process of trying to regain custody of them when she came to us for a free pregnancy test. She told us in the very first interview that she definitely could not go through with an abortion, yet she absolutely could not have another baby. We talked with her about the loving option of adoption, and she chose to give her baby to a family.

Because Leta wasn't sure who the father was, the ethnicity of the child was in question. Leta had to find an agency who could provide an adoptive couple who could accept and love her baby regardless of the unknown factors in the situation. The first couple that Leta selected from the profiles that the agency provided decided that they couldn't deal with the uncertainty, and that adoption fell through with only a few months left in the pregnancy.

Just a short time before the baby was due, the agency found

a couple who would be thrilled to adopt Leta's child, no matter what. The counselor at the adoption agency arranged for Leta to meet the couple at a restaurant. After meeting the couple, Leta knew that God had brought her these parents who would love and cherish her child. Even though the time was short until the baby's arrival, Leta and the adoptive parents managed to spend some time together. Leta requested that the adoptive parents be in the delivery room with her. As the final moments of labor approached, Leta says she felt the most love and support of her whole lifetime!

As the doctor finished the delivery, he looked up at Leta and said, "You are an amazing, strong and beautiful woman, and I admire you very much." The doctor handed the baby to her, and Leta gazed into the baby's sleepy eyes. She looked up at the adoptive parents and handed the baby to the proud new father. There wasn't a dry eye in that delivery room as those gathered witnessed Leta giving the greatest gift of all – the gift of life!

Hope Pregnancy Centers
Broward County, Florida

Heroes

Heroes don't need to be famous; they just need to be willing to save the lives of others. That is why birth mothers who place their babies for adoption are even more heroic than famous sports figures. They are willing to give life to babies who will not even belong to them after they're born.

All birth mothers have the option of adoption. Sometimes, birth mothers may even be influenced to abort by their husband, boyfriend, close friends or even parents. Birth mothers could also lose some of their friends for making the choice to give birth and place the baby for adoption. It takes a lot of bravery to say no to any of those people.

Birth mothers are also willing to share their life during pregnancy. If birth mothers don't eat right, or if they use drugs, the baby could be seriously injured or die. While birth mothers are attached to their baby, they are sharing their food and blood with it. That means birth mothers give about one third of their food and around two liters of blood to sustain their baby's life.

When birth mothers have their baby when they are young, or before they are married, that means they are willing to put up with the stigma and judgment of other people. Some people will judge birth mothers unfairly for the rest of their lives. Sometimes it's the parents of the birth mother that do the most judging, which is even more difficult.

Birth mothers ignore them all, just so they can give life to a baby. Birth mothers place their babies for adoption when they know their baby could be in a bad environment otherwise. The reasons are because they can't handle a baby physically, mentally or emotionally. Sometimes they are not married, and they don't want to raise a baby by themselves; or if their boyfriend does not want to get married, they don't want their baby not to have a father.

When birth mothers are choosing who should be their

child's parents, they look for people who are loving, live in a good environment and are financially secure. Most birth mothers also want to make sure that there is a father. They know that it's one of the most important decisions that they will make because it determines how successful their child's life will be.

Birth mothers do all this just to give their babies as a gift. Birth mothers have given their child the greatest gift on heaven and earth: the gift of life with opportunity. Birth mothers might not be famous or even popular, but they are most definitely the greatest heroes on the earth.

My birth mother is one of those heroes because she placed me for adoption when she was fourteen years old.

~ Brandon Lewis

Used with permission: A Woman's Friend 11/13/03
                       616 E. St.
                       Marysville, Ca. 95901
                       530-741-9136

AN OPEN ADOPTION

When we began the adoption process we were told it wasn't for the fainthearted. We have found this to certainly be true. What we weren't told was the gamut of emotions we would experience. In a twenty-four hour period we could feel joy, fear, excitement, doubt, happiness, uncertainty and every other emotion one can possibly imagine. When another couple was selected by a birth mother, we were happy for them, but wondered why not us. Did we come across as good people or would we never be chosen? All of these fears and doubts disappeared the moment I held our child.

Our son was born in October of 2004. He is now the center of our lives. Hearing his laughter or seeing his beautiful smile makes everything we went through seem insignificant. In many ways, ours was the perfect adoption.

We were fortunate enough to meet both birth parents and have stayed in touch with the mother. Hopefully, seeing how much we love our son and seeing him thrive helps her know she made the right decision. My son has siblings who, should he chose, he will be able to meet when he is older. We have complete health histories and most importantly, he will be able to understand that his biological parents made the most unselfish choice they could make.

It was never an issue of being unwanted; they simply were unable to provide the life they wanted him to have. One of the things that makes me most angry as an adoptive parent is for someone to tell me they could never "give up" their child. My response is that it takes a very loving parent to love so much that they are willing to sacrifice their wants and desires for the sake of their child; so he can have an opportunity for a much better life - a life they were unable to give him. This is the choice my child's biological parents made and I will be eternally grateful to them.

There were many steps between making our decision to

adopt and bringing our son home. Paperwork, paperwork and more paperwork initially. There were physicals and home studies and criminal background checks and references and, and, and...After all of this was completed and approved, came the hardest part, waiting.

What felt like an eternity was actually only a few months. We were very fortunate. We brought our precious son home only seven months after making the initial call to the agency. We truly believe that our adoption was God's plan for us and for our son. Most domestic adoptions do take longer. At the time we adopted our child, the average wait was less than a year at the agency - Adoptions of Kentucky, Louisville, Kentucky - we used. Unfortunately many people believe it takes years and don't even consider domestic adoption as an option.

We were chosen by our biological mother about six weeks before our child was due. We talked to both biological parents on the phone several times and then met them for dinner. His biological father was unsure about the adoption. It was very difficult to consider strangers raising his child. He did vacillate at times *which was beyond frightening!*

In fact, the night before our son was born he decided against the adoption. I can't begin to describe how devastated we were. I think if we had known our son would be born the next day, we both would have fallen apart. Our son wasn't due for three weeks so we thought we would have time to talk to his biological father again.

When his biological mother called me the next day and told me she was in labor, we didn't know what to do. Did we go knowing there was a very good chance we would come home alone? How much more difficult would it be for us to see the baby knowing he wouldn't be ours? In the end, we decided to just go and let God work things out. As Christians we both knew this was the only way we would be able to do this. We had to put it in God's hands.

We did not reach the hospital in time for the birth. Our son's birth mother had to have an emergency c-section. When we finally reached the hospital, we didn't get to see the baby for what seemed a lifetime. He was in the NICU because he had some minor respiratory issues. I can remember pacing the hallway just waiting to catch a glimpse of him. Seeing him and not being able to touch him was absolute torture. When I finally held him, I knew he was my child regardless of genetics!

The hospital was rather small and had obviously rarely, if ever, dealt with an open adoption. No one quite knew what to do with us. We slept on the floor in the waiting room because there was nowhere else for us; I wore the same clothes for two days. One of the nurses had adopted a child, and she was our advocate when our social worker wasn't there. It was uncomfortable at times; we were grateful for her.

Our birth mother graciously included us in every decision and gave us free access to our son. In fact, the second night I slept in her room although my husband was still on the waiting room floor! Each of the doctors involved was very receptive to us as adoptive parents which made things much easier.

We still didn't know if the birth father was going to agree to the adoption, and the three of us were literally sick to our stomachs. Again, God took control!

When the father came to the hospital to see the baby, he immediately told us he was going to sign the papers. He had a few, very reasonable requests. We assured him these were not a problem. We were more than happy to agree to these things. He never again seemed to doubt his decision. When it came time to terminate parental rights we went to his home to make things less awkward. We took pictures of him with our son and he made sure we had any information we might need if our son wants to contact him when he is older. He lives on the other side of the country now; so we have little contact. He calls on occasion, and we send him pictures.

Although an open adoption is probably not right for everyone, it has been a perfect fit for us.

The hardest moments were when we left the hospital with our baby. It was very difficult for his biological mother to leave without him. It was emotional for everyone involved. There were very few dry eyes. I could feel her pain, and in some ways I felt very guilty. *We were so happy, but at such a cost to another person.* I had to keep telling myself that it truly was the best thing for our son, and that was her goal. I know she loves him as much as I do and when I try to put myself in her shoes, I literally hurt physically! We will always owe her a debt of gratitude that we can never repay.

The finalization of our adoption went very smoothly. The final papers were signed sixty days after his birth, and our family was complete. He is such a blessing and having him in our lives is worth anything and everything we experienced. He is happy and healthy. This is all any of us wanted. People often tell us what a lucky little boy he is. What they don't realize is we consider ourselves to be the really lucky ones!

Pam and Jeff Ward
Paducah, Kentucky

STACY'S STORY

My story is one that you will hear over and over again if you spend much time inside a pregnancy center. But I will continue to tell it, hoping that it will touch the lives of girls like me. I will continue to tell it, hoping it will help parents continue to teach their daughters the truth about life. I will continue to tell it, hoping that it will give other girls the wisdom to make better choices than I made. I will continue to tell it, hoping it will give women the courage to make sacrificial decisions in the face of unplanned pregnancies. And I will continue to tell it, hoping that the Christian community will learn how to treat the women in their churches who stumble and fall.

Abortion is something that I definitely contemplated. There were days when I was driving in my car, crying so hard I couldn't see the road in front of me. I just wanted it to be over.

I was a senior in college and just about to graduate when I found myself in an unplanned pregnancy. I'd been with my boyfriend for almost three years. If you had told me back then "you're going to get pregnant and you will have to walk through it all by yourself," I would have laughed in your face. No way that could happen to me – we were always "careful" and we were in love. *He would always be there for me, no matter what.*

When I realized that I would be making the decisions about this baby alone, I went to the local pregnancy center that my church had helped start. I wanted to know about all my options. I also went on behalf of my parents. They needed for someone to tell us that this was going to be okay – that we were going to make it through this experience in spite of the disappointment and the pain.

The pregnancy center was a place that felt safe to me. I didn't feel judgment, which was a good thing, because I was already judging myself. I knew that I was in a situation that was the result of my own poor choices. I was beating myself up

47

because I had been taught all my life about God's plan for sex. I walked out of the center that day thinking, "There IS hope. I can get through this." I knew it would be a tough road, but knowing that I had the support of experienced, caring people gave me confidence to face the future. They had helped so many other girls; I knew they could help me.

Abortion kept coming to my mind as a quick and easy solution to my problem, but I knew in my heart that it wasn't an option for me. All those years of hearing the truth in Sunday School and church were so much a part of who I was. I had walked away from some of those truths, but the Holy Spirit was at work in my life, bringing God's words to the forefront of my mind. There were days when I was just plain angry at myself because I couldn't choose abortion – but I am thankful for the love of God that "constrains us."

I continued to go to the pregnancy center and meet with the same counselor each week. She led me through a workbook that explored the differences between parenting and placing for adoption. I knew from the beginning that adoption was a viable option, but I just didn't know how to go about it. The time we spent together helped me see that an adoption plan would be the best option for me. My counselor helped me talk about it objectively. She listened and encouraged me to listen to God. She never pressured me into any kind of decision; she just kept telling me that she was very proud of me for choosing life for my baby.

I knew that I was not at the place in life where I wanted to be when I became a parent. It was extremely important to me that my child have a father. I decided to make an adoption plan for my baby and give her the gift of a stable, loving, Christian family. I was able to do that because of the help I got at the pregnancy center. They connected me to a wonderful adoption agency. The adoption counselor walked with me through the many, many difficult decisions that were ahead.

It's one thing to make an adoption plan when you are five,

48

six, seven months pregnant. It's quite another thing to carry it out on the day the baby is born, and you hold the child in your arms that you have carried under your heart for nine months! I got so much strength from both my counselor at the pregnancy center and my adoption agency counselor. They never minimized my pain, and they never rattled off the trite, meaningless platitudes that people commonly say – things like "It'll all be over soon – someday you'll forget all about it – it's for the best…" and on and on. Because the truth is, when you walk away from God's plan for your life, there are consequences. Some consequences last forever. Even though several years have passed now, I am not "over it." I will never "forget all about it." And it wasn't "for the best". Yes, it was a good decision for me to place my baby for adoption – but God's "best" is saving sex for marriage so that girls like me won't have to face the heartbreak that comes from having to make difficult decisions like this. His wonderful plan is for our protection!

Just a note at this point in my story to all of you dear "church people". I have many friends who are adopted children; I grew up in a church where many of my parents' friends adopted babies. The "church" knows how to celebrate life! I saw my mom go to the baby showers and I saw the welcome that these "chosen children" received. It was often even more extravagant and joyous that the celebrations for the "regular babies"!

But no one at my church seemed to know quite what to do with me. When it became apparent that I was pregnant, people began to ask questions: "boy or girl? What are you going to name him/her?"…etc., etc. When I told people I was placing for adoption, no one knew what to say. I got horrified stares and thoughtless comments: "How could you carry a baby for nine months and give it away?" – and other variations of the same. *I finally quit going to church because it hurt too much. Let me suggest that if you are ever in the position of taking part in a conversation like that, that you simply say, "That is a very*

49

courageous decision," or "What a blessing this baby will be to that family," or "I am so proud of you for choosing life." Don't heap more pain on someone during one of the most difficult times of their life!

The day I came home from the hospital was one of the most difficult days of my life. It was my first time without my baby in nine months and that reality was very hard for me to deal with. I was alone, and she was with her new family, which was exactly how I knew it was going to be – was supposed to be. I just never imagined how bad I would feel. The process of grieving comes in stages, and my counselors warned me that I would experience a variety of emotions as God moved me through this phase of my life.

In the beginning I felt so guilty! I felt guilty for not parenting – I felt guilty for moving on with my life – I felt guilty for returning to a pursuit of my goals and dreams. I felt guilty for feeling happy! I thought that since I didn't have her in my life, I should just mope around for the rest of my life in sadness and despair.

God doesn't just wave a magic wand over us and say, "Well, since you've asked me for forgiveness, I'm just going to take all the consequences away and you'll live pain free forever!" The consequences of my actions were still there. His plan was for me to grow closer to Him as I worked through the healing process. He wanted me to understand that He has a plan for my life – and for my baby's life. I might not have planned for her, but He did! Through His unfolding plan, I began to discover that life's true meaning is not found in religion, but in a vibrant, growing relationship with Jesus Christ.

Abortion was something I contemplated. But the very first thought I had when I saw her face was "Thank you, God, for not letting me choose abortion." Nobody loved that baby more on the day she was born than I did. I draw peace and satisfaction from the knowledge that I chose life.

50

I'm at peace today with the decision I made to place my baby for adoption. She has the life that I wanted her to have, and I have the life that I had hoped for. God is so good.

~ Stacy
Hope Pregnancy Centers
Broward County, Florida

P.S.

As God worked in Stacy's life, He called her to serve as an abstinence educator in a pregnancy care center ministry for a season. She had the opportunity to impact thousands of youth and young adults with the message of truth and God's forgiving love.

SAVED FROM ABORTION

"Call unto me, and I will answer thee, and show thee great and mighty things, which thou knowest not."

~Jeremiah 33:3 KJV~

IF I'M PREGNANT, I MUST HAVE AN ABORTION

She approached the window hesitantly, looking behind her to see if anyone were listening. "May I help you?" the receptionist asked quietly. She leaned into the window and whispered, "I think I need a pregnancy test." A few minutes later she sat across from a counselor and tearfully shared her story. She is a Christian. She is married. She believes abortion is wrong. The counselor struggled to understand the words that were muffled by tears…"b-but if I'm pregnant, I h-have to have an abortion."

Using an effective communication skill of *rephrasing,* the counselor repeated what she believed the young woman had just said, "Even though you believe abortion is wrong, you think that you would have one if you are pregnant." The client grimaced as though the words brought pain to her, but nodded her head affirmatively. The counselor asked the next question, "How does your husband feel about it?" A fresh wave of tears began and after several minutes, still looking down at her lap, the client whispered, "It may not be his baby…that's the problem."

In halting sentences, peppered with frequent breakdowns, the whole story came out. The marriage appeared to be over. She was lonely. She met someone – and even knowing it was wrong, she gave in to temptation one time. A few weeks later her husband called and asked if they could see a Christian marriage counselor. God was healing her marriage, which was her heart's desire, but now she feared that she might be pregnant by someone other than her husband. She was heartbroken by the sin she had committed against God, by the sin she had committed against her husband, and by the sin she was about to commit by having an abortion.

I John 1:9 says, "If we confess our sin, He is faithful and just to forgive us our sin and to cleanse us from all unrighteousness." That was the verse the counselor shared with this frightened young woman during that first visit. The pregnancy test was positive, but she left with her sin confessed and forgiven by God, a resolve to confess to her husband and ask for his help and forgiveness, and a resolve to carry the baby to term. The hard decision about who would raise the child would come later.

Our God IS faithful and just. The months went by, and they continued to see a marriage counselor. God restored the love they had for each other, and together they decided that after the baby's birth they would do DNA testing. If the baby were a result of the affair, they would place it for adoption in a loving Christian family. Difficult decision? Yes, but they both realized that sin carries consequences, and sometimes we have to face them and deal with them for a very long time. Their decision to choose life was the right thing to do.

We stayed in touch with them throughout the pregnancy and were elated when the DNA testing proved that the baby belonged to her husband! This little family has experienced the grace of God and is very grateful to Hope Pregnancy Centers for helping them find their way through a very difficult time in their lives. They are thankful for the good and perfect gift of the child that God gave them through a true crisis pregnancy. Nothing is too difficult for God!

Hope Pregnancy Centers
Broward County, Florida

HIS LOVE REACHING

*"This day I call heaven and earth as witnesses against you that I have set before you life and death, blessings and curses. **Now choose life** that you and your children may live and that you may love the LORD your God, listen to his voice, and hold fast to him. For the LORD is your life, and he will give you many years in the land he swore to give to your fathers, Abraham, Isaac and Jacob."* ~*Deuteronomy 30:19-20 NIV*

They call and ask questions: **"How much are your abortions?"…"Do you have the morning-after pill?"…** "Can I get RU486 at one of your centers?"

Our goal is to get them to come into one of the centers where we can minister to them, face to face. We want to look them in the eye and speak the truth to them in love. We want to be the physical hands and feet of Christ as His love reaches into their hearts and lives.

But sometimes they can't or won't come in. Those are the times we have to trust Him to send His love reaching through the telephone lines.

It was a situation like this that one of our Center Directors shared with me a few weeks ago. She took a call from a young woman who wanted a chemical abortion procedure that is commonly called "RU486." As our Director asked some gentle, probing questions, she discovered that this telephone client was very strongly abortion-minded. She was not ambivalent about the pregnancy at all – she wanted to end it. Our counselor asked for permission to share some of the physical, emotional and spiritual ramifications of abortion. The girl listened, but was still firm in her resolve to terminate the pregnancy.

The Director sent up a prayer and pled, "Father, help me. How do I keep her on the line and try to find some common ground?" She felt the answer come quickly, *"Ask her if she knows what I think about abortion."* Taking a deep breath, our well-trained counselor forged ahead, "This may seem like a strange question, but do you believe in God?" The client's answer came back quickly, too: **"Oh, yes!"**

The next course of action became clearer to our Center Director, as she yielded to the leading of the Holy Spirit. "Do you have a Bible there in the house with you?" The client replied, "Yes, of course, I have a Bible. Bold now, the next question was easy, "Would you be willing to go and get it and read something to me from it?" Curious, the client agreed to go and get her Bible. A moment later she was back on the line, explaining that her text was in a foreign language, but she could translate if the Center Director did not speak the foreign language. [God has such a sense of humor in the way He often does things! ☺]

"Go to Deuteronomy 30:19-20 and read that to me," the Center Director instructed. The young woman on the other end of the phone line read the words in her native language and was totally silent. After a moment passed, the counselor gently asked, "Now, can you explain to me in English what that says?" With a catch in her voice and an attitude of awe, the client said, "I think that I have just discovered that God says choose life, and that I don't really believe in abortion after all."

His love is continually reaching...even through the telephone lines!

Hope Pregnancy Centers
Broward County, Florida

NO EASY CHOICES

We never underestimate the difficult decisions our clients face when they find themselves in an unplanned pregnancy. There are no easy choices when people's lives hang in the balance.

But there **are** choices, and we encourage them to choose life at every turn: life for the child they carry and new life in Christ for themselves. LIFE is a wonderful choice and it makes a difference for all eternity!

Please pray for our staff. Every day we receive more and more phone calls from abortion-minded clients. When they understand that we do not provide abortions, many of them simply hang up. We try very hard to engage them in conversation and offer them an opportunity to come in for a free pregnancy test and talk with us about their situation, but many simply will not come in.

Hardened hearts are a sign of the times we live in, but those of us who are on the front lines must stay focused on the hope that is found in Christ and Christ alone. It is especially difficult for our center directors and the volunteers who counsel these young women who are literally making decisions about life and death.

Our greatest joy is when one of these "hard cases" is rescued by the love of God, which is being liberally poured out in those little counseling rooms all over our country. One of our directors recently told me the following story. I hope you will rejoice as you read it.

"I remember the first time I saw her. She wasn't really what I would call a high-risk for abortion. She mentioned it in the first interview as something she had thought about, but said she had a good support system if she chose to carry. Her mother would help take care of the baby while she finished school and the baby's father said he would provide financial support. I gave her a referral for medical services and by the third time I saw her, she

had qualified for Medicaid. It was one of those situations where I thought, "Whew! That one is out of the woods!"

I learned later that she did have other children and that she was in a desperate situation financially. The subject of abortion came up again, but when I shared information with her about fetal development and placed a tiny fetal model of a twelve-week baby in her hand, she wept and agreed that she could not destroy the developing life within her. She missed her next appointment with me, but rescheduled another, and then missed that one, too.

I had permission to call her, so I did call to express my compassion for the difficulties she was having. She took a deep breath and spoke very quickly, "Oh, it's going to be okay...I finally made up my mind and I am having the abortion." I felt like ice water had been pumped into my veins, and I fought the temptation to react by screaming, "NO, don't do it!" Instead, I quietly asked for permission to call her again. I told her I would continue to pray for her. Amazingly, she gave me permission to call, and we said good-bye.

I prayed and prayed for her, but when I attempted to contact her again, her phone was disconnected. I continued to pray, but I had a hard time shaking the feeling of despair that fell on me. More than two months went by, and I did not hear from her again.

I took a call from a social worker a few days ago and was told that she was working with a young woman who had planned on having an abortion, but had changed her mind. She wondered if we might be able to help. I agreed to make an appointment to see the agency's client who now needed maternity clothes and help with baby items as her pregnancy advanced. When I heard the name the social worker spoke into the phone, I wanted to jump up and down! It was **she**! God had spared that baby's life, and in His mysterious way had used a public social service agency to steer her right back into our hands!

She wasn't aware of which agencies the social worker was

contacting on her behalf! When the social worker heard the excitement in my voice, she put the client on the phone with me. I was able to assure her that I really had been praying for her every day. She was encouraged by seeing how He had led her back to Hope, and I was encouraged to see the great lengths He had gone to in order to protect the life of this precious one. He DOES have plans for a hope and a future for EVERY LIFE!
~ Jeremiah 29:11

Hope Pregnancy Centers
Broward County, Florida

TOO FAR ALONG TO HAVE AN ABORTION

"I just couldn't believe it when the doctor's assistant came into the room and told me I was too far along to have the abortion." ~ a client

The client told us she had agonized over what to do and had finally decided that abortion was the only solution to her unplanned pregnancy. She scheduled an appointment at a local clinic and went in to have the pregnancy terminated.

After a routine sonogram, she was informed that she was 24 ½ weeks pregnant and that in the physician's opinion, an abortion at this stage of pregnancy would be dangerous. [*Praise God for this physician...there are some who would have gone ahead and done this late-term abortion in a county where, ironically, just a few miles away one of the best neo-natal units in the country routinely saves babies who are prematurely born at 24 ½ weeks!*]

She walked out thinking, "What will I do now?" Someone told her about Hope Pregnancy Centers.

By the time we met this client, she was ready to listen to life-affirming options. She told us that after she saw the sonogram, she "connected" to her baby. As she shared with us about her life, we learned that she had accepted Christ as her Savior at age eleven, but had stopped walking with Him in recent years.

We helped her understand that He still loved her and still had a wonderful plan for her life – a plan with hope and a future. She rededicated her life to Jesus. She is anticipating the arrival of her baby very soon. She isn't alone and afraid anymore. She knows she has friends at Hope who love her and will encourage her and help her in the weeks and months ahead.

What a mighty God we serve! He even used an abortionist to save this baby's life. **Do you understand how solid the ground we stand on is??** Do you see how we were able to proclaim confidently to this client – and to every client – *"There's **nothing** that can separate us from the love of Christ! Not trouble, not hardship, not persecution or famine or nakedness or* danger or *sword..."* [nor unplanned pregnancy, nor abortionist's knife]...No, *"in ALL these things we are more than conquerors through Him who loved us. For WE are convinced that neither death nor life, neither angels nor demons, neither the present nor the future, nor any powers, neither height nor depth, nor anything else in all creation, will be able to separate us from the love of God that is in Christ Jesus our Lord." ~ Romans 8:35-39*

Hope Pregnancy Center
Broward County, Florida

I HAVE TO KILL MY BABY

"Seek the kingdom of God, and all these things shall be added to you. Do not fear, little flock, for it is your Father's good pleasure to give you the kingdom." ~Luke 12:31-32

Nadia could barely speak English. The only thing the counselor could understand was that she desperately wanted an abortion. There was no confusion…her broken words were clear "I have to kill my baby." She was of the Muslim faith. She knew it was morally wrong, but her face was set to ending her baby's life. We held her hands; we cried with her; we made another appointment and she left.

Through a miraculous chain of events that humans could have never orchestrated, God provided a Christian, pro-life interpreter (who has been a faithful supporter of Hope for twelve years!) who spoke Nadia's strange middle-eastern dialect AND who was free to come in the afternoon of Nadia's next appointment!

As the story was amplified through understanding the language, we learned that Nadia and her husband had just come to America. They had hopes and dreams of pursuing success in a land that was free. They encountered many difficulties that they did not anticipate, and were not experiencing life as they imagined it would be. They wanted to have children – someday – when they were well established and ready.

When Nadia discovered she was pregnant, she felt miserable. Her husband insisted that in their present circumstance, there was no way to have a baby. All of those reasons led her to the conclusion that she must have an abortion, **BUT GOD** moved in her heart.

After that first appointment with us, she called an abortion clinic and scheduled an abortion. She went to that appointment. **BUT GOD** would not allow her to see it through. She says

65

"something" inside her told her to get up and go back to Hope. That was the day He provided an interpreter for her.

Today Nadia and her husband are the VERY PROUD parents of a bouncing baby boy. We have had the privilege of helping them because of the generosity of our donors. We have baby clothes and diapers to give to them. We have had furniture donated to us that we could not use in our offices that we have been able to give to help them furnish their apartment. We have had the privilege, through our home visitation ministry, to be in their home and become part of their lives. Bettie, our home visitation director, assisted at the birth!

Lives intertwined…that is our hope. We are still praying that they come to a full, saving knowledge of Jesus Christ. They are very open to hear the Gospel. They ask   lots of questions. Pray for them, and for us, as we continue to minister to them.

Have no doubt that all of us here at Hope know that God is the author – and the finisher – of each and every story! *We have often said that we make a difference "one life at a time" – we are seeing more clearly every day that it is frequently TWO lives at a time!*

Hope Pregnancy Centers
Broward County, Florida

NEVER ALONE

One of my favorite responsibilities as Executive Director is my monthly meeting with our Client Services Director, and all of the Center Directors. We sit around the table and they share the real life stories of what God is doing in the small centers He has placed in Broward County, Florida.

The theme that emerges month after month is that when a counselor enters the counseling room with a client, there are always unseen guests who enter the room with them! NEVER ALONE is a phrase that is repeated over and over…the Holy Spirit is there, leading the conversation and a Heavenly Host of angels surrounds the counselor and client during each divine appointment. The following story, as told to me by one of our Center Directors, is just a glimpse of what God can do in one brief hour – and is a reminder that as we fight the battle for life, we are NEVER ALONE.

"When I opened the door to invite her to come with me, she reminded me of a deer who is caught in the blinding glare of the headlights. I wasn't sure if she would bolt and run away from me or if she might charge and knock me down. Her big eyes were wide with apprehension as she moved slowly to follow me into the counseling room.

As I began to complete the intake form, it became clear to me that she was very nervous and very concerned about confidentiality. She did not give me a phone number and I suspected that the name and address she gave me were fictitious.

She told me she was considering an abortion because she didn't want to tell her family that she was pregnant. When I asked her how her boyfriend felt about a possible pregnancy, she told me he would support whatever decision she made. I understood that she felt truly alone.

After I talked with her a little more, she did the pregnancy test. We both sat silently for a few minutes as she stared at the positive test result. She reiterated her need to get an abortion. She said she didn't really have any other choice.

I asked her some questions about her situation and her family. I noticed that she began to calm down. I asked her if she believed in God. When she said yes, I moved quickly through that open door and asked for permission to share with her some of the physical, emotional and spiritual aspects of abortion.

She listened politely, but when we got to the spiritual aspect of abortion, she really tuned in. I looked up Jeremiah 1:5 and asked her to read it aloud. ["Before I formed you in the womb I knew you, before you were born I set you apart; I appointed you as a prophet to the nations."] I turned back to Deuteronomy 30:19-20 and asked her to read again. ["This day I call heaven and earth as witnesses against you that I have set before you life and death, blessings and curses. Now choose life, so that you and your children may live and that you may love the LORD your God, listen to his voice, and hold fast to Him. For the LORD is your life, and He will give you many years in the land He swore to give to your fathers, Abraham, Isaac and Jacob."]

God spoke to her through His Word, and it became obvious to her that He would not be in favor of an abortion. She confessed that she already had a sense that it would be the wrong thing to do, but was pushing those thoughts away. She knew she had a choice to go God's way or her own way.

We talked about how a baby would change her life. She began to relax and even laughed a few times. We definitely had connected.

I explained our confidential calling procedure, and told her I would like to have permission to call her to follow up. When she understood that we had a secure line that would not show up on a caller ID, she gave me her phone number. With a sheepish grin, she added, " Let me give you my real address, too."

The walls came down; she trusted me! It was a great moment. I have talked to her several times since that day and her pregnancy is going well. She decided God's way was best. I am glad that I am NEVER ALONE in the counseling room. I certainly felt the presence of the Holy Spirit and the angels on that day!

Nancy McDonald
Executive Director
Hope Pregnancy Centers
Broward County, Florida

FREEDOM THAT GUARANTEES PEACE

Jesus said, "If you hold to my teachings, you are really my disciples. Then you will know the truth, and the truth will set you free." ~ John 8:32 NIV

During the month of July there is a lot of talk about freedom in our country. The rhetoric will continue through the summer months as the political machinery is put in motion, focusing on the fall elections. Everybody talks about freedom, but few experience what God intended when He spoke of freedom in His Word. Abiding by His truth is where we find true freedom – the freedom that guarantees peace.

Sue came to our center over fifteen years ago, hoping to find someone who would encourage her to exercise her "freedom" to choose abortion as the solution to her unplanned pregnancy. Instead, she found a friend who loved her enough to tell her the truth. Sue's counselor told her the truth about abortion and the physical, emotional and spiritual risks that she would face in its aftermath. Sue chose life. As the baby Sue carried grew in her womb, the friendship between Sue and her counselor grew, too.

One day, Sue trusted Jesus as her Savior and began a journey that would last a lifetime.

In the early years, Sue stayed in close contact with her counselor. The pregnancy center was an ongoing source of comfort and support for Sue as her little boy grew. But then Sue got busy, her counselor had other clients to see, and the time stretched between visits from Sue. A phone call here and there, a note, a card and it wasn't long before Sue became a story from our history book.

The faces of the volunteers and staff members change and life goes on as new clients come in and their needs are met.

The phone rang the other day and a woman asked, "Is Ann still a counselor there?" Ann was still there and the young woman was so excited! She wanted to tell us the "rest of the story." Sue shared with Ann about how God had worked in her life over the past fifteen years to bring her to Himself.

Her story unfolded as she shared how she had struggled in her faith in the early years following her conversion at Hope. She told Ann how hard it was to find a church that would accept a single mother without judgment or condemnation. Then God led her to a congregation that loved her, embraced her and encouraged her.

She got her education and that degree led to a career that was fulfilling and allowed her to support her son. Her son had already accepted Christ as his Savior, and at age fifteen, he feels God calling him to full-time ministry. Now mature in her faith, Sue knew Ann would love to know all that had happened as a result of Ann's obedience to share Jesus in that counseling room so long ago.

Sue called to thank Ann and Hope Pregnancy Centers for all we had done for her when she was in distress and struggling with her 'freedom to choose.' She wants her son to come in and meet Ann! I am sure she would like to personally thank each one of our donors if she could, for giving to our ministry so that we could be there fifteen years ago to help her and still be here today to help girls like her.

On behalf of all the "Sues" who are coming into our centers on a daily basis, I thank all of those who support pregnancy care centers. The stories go on and on. Life IS a beautiful choice!

Hope Pregnancy Centers
Broward County, Florida

"I don't like counselors.
I don't like Christians.
I don't trust anybody"

She is in middle school. Yes, *middle school* – and pregnant. She was being pulled on one side by the boyfriend and his family to abort ~ and encouraged by her own Christian parents to choose life. She attends a school with a strict behavior code, and she knows that she will be expelled if they find out she is pregnant. There is no written policy about abortion, so it seems like a smart choice ~ an easy way out ~ to these two frightened, confused young people.

Her first visit occurred on a day that we should have been closed. Mechanical difficulties in the plaza where our center is located made closing a necessity for most of the businesses. After the counselor talked to this young client on the telephone, she made a decision to keep the center open. The phone interview began with the quote from above: *"I don't like counselors; I don't like Christians. I don't trust anybody."*

The counselor wasn't even confident that she would show up for the appointment, but just a few hours later she came in with one of her parents. The session wasn't exactly what we would call a success, but she did agree to come back and bring her boyfriend the next night when one of our male counselors would be available.

It is a wonderful thing to walk in the shadow of the Most High God. They came in the next day and watched a video together. After the video, the young man went into the counseling room with one of our men and was challenged to accept his responsibility as a father by encouraging this young woman to choose life. He walked out of that little room an hour later with a changed heart. He recognized that he was already a father, and he was ready to help his girlfriend carry their baby to term.

In the other counseling room, a confused little girl gained enough courage to voice some of her concerns. *"What if I get kicked out of school?"* Our counselor told her that there were alternative programs for education for pregnant teens.

"I don't know anything about having a baby or being a parent." Our counselor assured her that we would encourage her, support her, give her good information, and refer her to competent professionals who could help her.

"Where will I get the money to buy all the stuff you need for a baby?" Our counselor was glad to be able to tell her that we would be able to help provide for her needs from our abundantly stocked donation room. Her response was immediate – and somewhat belligerent: "Show me." We don't recall anyone ever asking that before, but she was taken down the hallway to see the bounty that God has given to us to share with our clients.

There in the doorway of a room filled with cribs, car seats, diapers, formula, and baby clothing, she was overshadowed by the God of the Universe. She had to see the "stuff". She has decided to carry her baby to term. She asked the counselor to stay in touch with her.

Hope Pregnancy Centers
Broward County, Florida

74

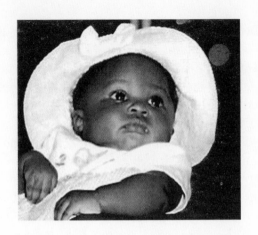

TWO LIVES SAVED

"Answer me, O Lord, out of the goodness of your love; in your great mercy turn to me. Do not hide your face from your servant; answer me quickly, for I am in trouble. Come near and rescue me; redeem me because of my foes." Psalms 69:16-18 NIV

She came into the center with a heavy heart. She needed a pregnancy test, but she did not want to be pregnant. She told the counselor that her boyfriend would probably want her to have the baby if the test were positive, but there was no one else in her life who would support the idea of her having a baby – and certainly no one in her life who would help her raise a child. She was very close to her sister, and she knew that her sister would definitely pressure her to have an abortion if she were pregnant.

The counselor explained to her exactly what happens in an abortion. She shared good, truthful information with the young woman and then provided the pregnancy test. When the client read the result of the pregnancy test as positive, she was very upset. She cried out for help – she knew she was in the worst trouble of her young life.

God heard her cry for help and provided a loving, caring counselor to tell her about the free gift of salvation provided in Jesus' life, death, and resurrection. She listened attentively and eagerly prayed to receive Christ when the opportunity was provided. She was very sincere and seemed to have a very clear understanding of the decision she had made. She took the Bible that was offered. As they continued to talk about the Lord and the wonderful plans He had for her life, she made a very courageous decision to carry the baby.

Months later, she told us that she had made a real commitment to the Lord that day. She knew that He had *shown His face to her, had answered her quickly, and had come near to be a help in her time of trouble. He had surely rescued her.* She gave birth to a beautiful baby girl and continues to remain in contact with us.

Please know that when you give to a pregnancy care center you help save two lives. This baby's life was saved from abortion. This mother's life was saved for all eternity. Today another client will open the door and come to us in desperate need. Our donors allow us to be here to offer life to the unborn children and new life to their moms and dads.

Hope Pregnancy Centers
Broward County, Florida

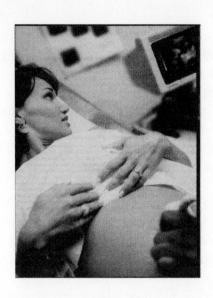

THE SANCTITY OF HUMAN LIFE
as observed by King David

For you created my inmost being;
You knit me together in my mother's womb.
I praise you because I am fearfully and
Wonderfully made; your works are wonderful,
I know that full well. My frame was not hidden
From you when I was made in the secret place.
When I was woven together in the depths of
The earth, your eyes saw my unformed body.
All the days ordained for me were written in
Your book before one of them came to be.
                              ~Psalms 139:13-16

The technology of our day is amazing, isn't it? Remember when you had to wait for the baby to be born to know if it were a girl or a boy? Today expectant moms can look through the "window of the womb" via the sonogram machine and bond with their baby months before the doctor or nurse places the tiny bundle in their arms.

Recently a client came to us and told us how technology had saved the life of her unborn child. She was pregnant, alone and scared. She didn't know where to turn. Her friends said that she would be crazy to have a baby. They assured her that abortion was quick, safe and easy – the perfect solution to her problem. She called a local abortion clinic and scheduled an appointment.

When the clinic sonographer performed the routine ultrasound, the client inadvertently saw the monitor. (Usually the monitors in abortion clinics are turned away from the client so that she does not see the screen.) This one was divinely positioned and this young woman saw the truth that King David knew only by faith – the computer monitor didn't reveal a mass of tissue…it revealed an active human baby! Even before the abortion doctor told her that she was almost twenty-five weeks pregnant and that the abortion would be high-risk, she knew that she could not destroy this baby's life.

Seeing the sonogram provided a bond between this mother and her child that was not to be broken by abortion. Her situation is still very difficult, but she is carrying the baby to term. As the peer counselor shared the Good News of Jesus Christ, the client told about a time in her life when she had gone to church and had invited Jesus into her heart. She admitted that she had walked away from her relationship with the Lord a very long time ago. The counselor talked about the wonderful plan that God had for her life. This young woman prayed and asked Jesus to once again take control of her life. Pray for her to remain true to His calling on her life.

This is the second client we have seen in the last three months who has been turned away from an abortion clinic because of her advanced pregnancy. Praise God for the great lengths He goes to in order to save these little ones! Praise God that at least two abortionists were unwilling to do these late-term abortions. Pray for God to have mercy on our nation and stop abortion.

Hope Pregnancy Centers
Broward County, Florida

THANK YOU!

A Few Words From Kemy:
"Thank you so much for your encouragement. I don't know what I would do without Nita...I am so glad I didn't have an abortion. I'm glad basically that God led me to Hope – I just didn't know what I was going to do when I found out I was pregnant."

Before she came to the pregnancy center, Kemy had visited an abortion clinic. They told her she was about twenty-two weeks pregnant. She had every intention of having an abortion but agreed to seek some counsel first, due to the advanced stage of her pregnancy. She was filled with fear and doubt. She was afraid that her boyfriend would be upset; that she would end up with no money, no job, no place to live, and no babysitter.

We listened to her story, encouraged her to seek God's wisdom and prayed with her. Kemy agreed to come back and see us before returning to the clinic.

Kemy continued to see her counselor at Hope on a regular basis and the weeks grew into months. Her "decision" evolved into a baby. We helped her with maternity clothes and later many beautiful baby clothes and other baby items.

Little Nita was born healthy and beautiful. She has been a frequent visitor to the center. Kemy continues to thank us on each visit for talking to her about good options and for helping to guide her to the decision to give life for Nita.

Kemy's boyfriend returned to the area and fell in love with little Nita. He is committed to being a good father. He and Kemy are married now, have their own apartment and are attending church. Grandma baby sits during the day so her son can work to provide for his family. He and Kemy both obtained good jobs with the same company. They are working hard to get out of debt. They have both received promotions already! Kemy exhibited her love and appreciation for her counselor by asking her to be one of Nita's godmothers. (Of course, the counselor said YES!)

God was faithful to answer our prayers for Kemy – and in case you didn't pick up on it – He alleviated every fear and concern that Kemy brought to us during that first visit! I guess He meant it when He said, *"For I know the plans I have for you – plans to prosper you and not to harm you; plans to give you hope and a future." (Jeremiah 29:11)*

Don't you just love the way God lets us be involved in the work He is doing in the world?

Hope Pregnancy Centers
Broward County, Florida

MARRIAGE JUST DOESN'T WORK

June – the month of "School's Out!, Happy Father's Day, and **beautiful brides'** – a month of celebration and joy for many families. But June is a month of heartbreak and disillusionment for many women who find themselves in an unplanned pregnancy. When we first met "Darlene", she was one of those brokenhearted, disillusioned women.

She had two small children and was involved in a serious relationship with a man she was not married to. She came in for a free pregnancy test, but she did NOT want to be pregnant again. Even though her boyfriend said he was "okay" with another baby, she felt overwhelmed by the possibility of being pregnant again.

Abortion sounded like the only choice she would consider if the pregnancy test were positive. When the subject of marriage to the boyfriend was approached, she remembered the pain of her parents' divorce and shared it with us. She said bitterly, "Marriage just doesn't work, so why even bother?"

Our counselors are trained not to rush into the pregnancy test. Clients are given plenty of time to talk about their feelings and explore the options available to them before the pregnancy test is done. It was during this relaxed time of interaction that we learned that Darlene had been attending church and had recently made a profession of faith in Christ. With this new information, the counselor was able to center the conversation on the Scriptures and help Darlene understand God's viewpoint about life.

With the open Bible in her hand, Darlene read aloud from Deuteronomy 30:19-20: "This day I call heaven and earth as witnesses against you that I have set before you life and death, blessings and curses. Now choose life, so that you and your children may live and that you may love the LORD your God, listen to His voice, and hold fast to Him. For the LORD is your life, and He will give you many years in the land He swore to give to your fathers, Abraham, Isaac and Jacob."

With tears in her eyes, she took a deep breath and told the counselor, "I'm ready to do the pregnancy test now. I know what God wants me to do if I am pregnant."

The Scriptures had spoken to her heart. The test was positive. She thanked God for the child in her womb, promising Him she would choose life. She has started to see things from God's prospective, and is looking forward to the delivery date of her baby girl.

The wedding date hasn't been set just yet, but she and her boyfriend are seeing a Christian counselor…when the time is right, we trust God will help her make a wise choice in that area, too.

Because the private sector supports this ministry, we are free to share the gospel boldly. There are no constraints on our ability to share the truth of Scripture, because our brothers and sisters in Christ support this work.

Hope Pregnancy Centers
Broward County, Florida

THE LIFE CHAIN

Every year on the first Sunday in October, people from all denominations from all over the country come together in their own cities to form what is called the "Life Chain."

People gather on busy streets and span out to cover as much territory as possible. For one hour (from 2 – 3 PM) people come together to hold up signs. Some of the signs say, "Abortion Kills Children", others say, "Adoption, the Better Option", and "Jesus Forgives and Heals."

This is not a protest. It is simply telling people what abortion does – it kills babies; but there is forgiveness in Jesus Christ.

One year as we stood on University Drive, one of the very busy streets in Fort Lauderdale, Florida, a woman stopped, parked her car and walked up to one of our people who was holding a sign. She said, "I just had to stop and share this story with you. Last year when my daughter and I passed by here and you were holding signs, we read these signs over and over as we traveled south on University Drive. My daughter was pregnant at that time. She planned to have an abortion."

The woman reached into her purse and pulled out a picture of a beautiful baby girl.

"Thanks to people like you who are willing to do this, I now have a beautiful granddaughter. Thank you, thank you so much for saving my granddaughter's life."

This is only one story that I have heard. I am sure there are many more.

Sometimes people just need to be reminded that abortion does kill a "real" child.

Jeanetta Bearden Pollard

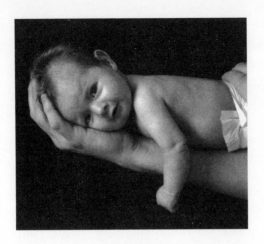

Laurie

School has started and there are reminders everywhere that the holidays are coming. Just stop in at your local discount store if you need to be convinced! They are tearing down the back-to-school displays and making room for the short-lived autumn season before the Christmas decorations take over completely. The months do fly quickly by! One of our center directors gave me this client story.

We just never know what the "hook" is that God will use to touch their hearts. Let me tell you about "Laurie" and ask you to pray for other clients like her that God will bring our way. Pray for us, too, that we will have our "hooks" ready and baited with exactly what each one needs to be caught for the kingdom!

"Laurie" came in while we were in the midst of choosing which clients should receive the Thanksgiving baskets that one of our churches had supplied. She was looking for an abortion. Her first pregnancy, as a teenager, had ended in abortion.

Just a short time after her abortion, a second pregnancy led to a hasty marriage. She had another baby before the marriage ended in divorce. By the time she came to the center, she was remarried and pregnant again. Her husband had lost his job, and she was the only wage earner in the family. She felt like another abortion was the only way out of this difficult situation.

We encouraged her to trust God and see if He would provide a way through the difficulties. We sent her out with some pretty maternity clothes and a Thanksgiving basket for her family. We learned that they had moved out of the area when we tried to follow-up with her. We continued to pray for God to protect the life she carried and to help her family in their trials.

Early in July, "Laurie" waddled through the door, nine months plus pregnant! She said she just wanted to stop in and say "thank you". The baby was due any minute and she wanted to share with us that she had seen God turn her situation from despair to hope.

She was happy and excited about the arrival of the new baby. She was so thankful that we had offered her hope and help.

We were able to continue to minister to "Laurie" and her family. We gave her some much-needed items for the new baby and the promise of more help if she needs us.

Some clients come looking for a handout... "Laurie" came back to thank us for giving her a hand UP.

Hope Pregnancy Centers
Broward County, Florida

DO YOU REMEMBER ME?
A Letter from a Center Director

I heard the bell ring and opened the window. A pretty young woman rushed up and smiled broadly. "Hi! Do you remember me?" she asked. I didn't want to hurt her feelings – and I did think she looked familiar, so I evaded the question.

"You look so familiar – but I can't put a name with your face...how can I help you?" By this time another young woman, an older woman, and a toddler had come into the reception area, and it was obvious that they were all together.

She glanced over her shoulder at them and lowered her voice, "Can I come in and talk with you?" Her tone was so serious – and desperate – that I didn't follow the protocol of having her fill out paperwork. I opened the door and invited her to sit with me in one of the counseling rooms.

She told me that she was my client three years earlier, and I had shared a Bible verse with her that convinced her to have her baby. I went to the file cabinet and pulled her file. She had been very abortion-minded when she came in three years ago, but in the end had chosen to give life to her little girl. The toddler in the waiting room was the saved baby! I listened...

Her story came out in a rush of words, "You have to talk to my sister. We just came back from the abortion clinic. I tried to talk her out of it, but she and my mom were determined to go through with it. I didn't even want to drive them there, but my mom has helped me so much that I couldn't figure out how to tell them no.

The most amazing thing happened at the clinic. They did an ultrasound and told her that she was further along than they had first thought – now it was a second trimester abortion and she needed more money. She didn't have it and they told her to get dressed and come back when she could pay the additional $200 fee. She made an appointment for three days later.

She came out crying and said, 'What do I do now?'...I remembered how you helped me three years ago, so here we are. You showed such love for me. You have to talk to her – tell her that verse you told me about choosing life! Do you remember that you closed the office to go with me to the electric company and pay my light bill? When everyone in my life told me to get an abortion, you told me that you would help me choose life. You have to help my sister – it's a miracle that she didn't already have the abortion!"

I did remember her. I remembered that she cried when I read Deuteronomy 30:19 to her. I remembered locking the door of the center and driving to the electric company, wondering if I were wasting the ministry's money in paying her electric bill. Would such an act of kindness really convince her to choose life for the child she carried?

I glanced over my notes from three years before and smiled when I read, "client indicated that she would carry to term." The bouncy little girl in the waiting room was physical evidence that paying the electric bill led to life! Now someone this young woman loved was on the verge of making a terrible mistake. She had brought her sister to the lighthouse called Hope...what a privilege I had to share truth with her!

Protocol went out the window that day as I brought the younger sister back to join us in the counseling room. There was no violation of confidentially – this was already an open family discussion. I asked the younger sister how she felt about what had happened at the clinic. She thought for a moment and then said a single word: "Relieved."

We talked at length about God's wonderful plan for her life. She confided that she had recently accepted Christ as her Savior when she went to church with her sister, but shortly thereafter had discovered she was pregnant. Satan had robbed her of her joy by accusing her and condemning her sin. Her primary thought was to escape the pregnancy, put the abortion behind her, and move on with her life. She was so open to hearing from God!

I shared Jeremiah 29:11 with her, *"For I know the plans I have for you," declares the Lord, "plans to prosper you and not to harm you; plans to give you a hope and a future."* The tears had already started to fall and when I opened the Bible to Deuteronomy 30:19-20 and asked her to read, she choked out the words, "This day I call heaven and earth as witnesses against you that I have set before you life and death, blessings and curses. Now choose life, so that you and your children may live and that you may love the Lord your God, listen to His voice, and hold fast to Him. For the Lord is your life, and He will give you many years in the land He swore to give to your fathers, Abraham, Isaac and Jacob."

It was silent in the room as the three of us pondered those words. After a few minutes, I asked her quietly, "What about that abortion appointment three days from now?"

"I can't do it."

How can four little words make your heart soar? How can four little words make you feel like a hero, a champion of life? I know that the almighty God had spoken to her heart – but I got to be there to witness the miracle of His work once again!

We talked a little more about a course of action for her to take, and they stood to leave. Big sister moved to embrace me and whispered a muffled "Thank you – thank you so much!" into my neck. I asked for permission to hug little sister, and she practically fell into my arms. I think she hugged me harder than anyone has ever hugged me before. She turned tear-filled eyes upon me, and her face was glowing with joy as she said, "You're gonna help lots of girls just like you've helped me."

I pray that her words prove to be prophetic. I look forward to the day when two little cousins come back to visit me.

Margy Richardson
A grateful center director
Hope Pregnancy Centers
Broward County, Florida

I HAVE BEEN SO BLESSED

She was young and her life was wonderful. She had a bright future planned that included a college degree and a successful career. During the winter semester, the flu was going around. One night she began to experience such severe stomach cramps that she asked her parents to take her to the emergency room.

In a tiny, green-draped cubicle she waited for the doctor to come in and prescribe medication that would relieve her pain. She was shocked when he said, "Did you know that you are pregnant?" Later, after we became her friends, she would tell us that in those few seconds a thousand thoughts rushed through her mind..."I can't be pregnant! This cannot be happening to me! We were 'careful'!... How can I walk out into that waiting room and tell my parents? They don't even know that I am sexually active...they will be so disappointed. My life is ruined – I can't have a baby!"...and on and on.

She asked the doctor not to say anything about the pregnancy to her parents, and she dried her tears as she went out of the hospital ~ with a firm resolve in her heart to get an abortion as soon as she could so that no one would know about the pregnancy, and she could 'get on with her life.'

She felt lonely and afraid. Somewhere in the darkness, there was the light of hope, leading her to find answers at a pregnancy care center. She doesn't remember how she found out about the local pregnancy care center, but one day she walked through the door, and God met her there.

The loving words of a caring counselor spoke words of life to her, and she decided to carry the baby. She renewed her commitment to the Lord Jesus Christ that day and has been growing in her faith ever since. That 'baby' is a busy, active ten-year-old boy now!

Not only have we been privileged to see him grow ~ we have been privileged to see his mother grow, too. Over the years she has given back to the pregnancy care center as a volunteer, as a donor, and as a part-time staff member.

That little boy attends a Christian school, and his mom returned to the classroom, too, to finish the work she had started before his birth. God didn't ask her to forfeit her college education to give life to her son...He just had a different timetable in mind. It pleases the Father to give us the desires of our hearts...it blesses us to see Him doing that in this young woman's life. We are so thankful to be involved in this 'continuing story' of God's faithfulness.

About three years ago, we received a wedding invitation. God had connected a wonderful young Christian man to this single mom and her little boy, someone who would love them both and be the kind of husband who would cherish her and protect her; someone who would be the kind of loving father whom growing little boys need. She met him at church, of course. God has a wonderful plan for every life, and it is such a blessing when we see our clients discover His plan!

Just last week, we received a letter from this very special client. Inside the envelope was a photograph of a beautiful baby boy. *"Every good and perfect gift is from above." [James 1:17]* Our God is an awesome God! He provided for every need in this client's life AND gave her gifts and blessings that go far beyond her wildest dreams and expectations. I talked to her on the phone the other day and her parting words to me were, "I have been SO blessed."

Hope Pregnancy Centers
Broward County, Florida

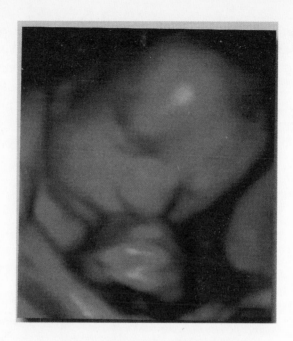

A LETTER TO GLENDA

Dear Glenda,

Hello. I know it has been a long time since we have talked, about five months to be precise. I met you when I visited Hope Pregnancy Center. I came there to find out how much it cost to have an abortion. I left that day with the knowledge that I had a little life growing inside of me.

I wasn't sure what to do or say. Well, you were kind enough to keep in touch with me and check on things. You even made the calls to get me an ultrasound and a doctor's appointment. But then my cell phone got turned off due to lack of payment and you and I lost touch. I am writing you now to tell you what has happened to me.

That day in the Center you talked to me about God, and you told me where you attended church. I hadn't gone to church a

94

whole lot in my life, but when I did attend, I went to that very same church – remember? That is actually where I met my boyfriend, who is now the father of my baby. Then I found out that the doctor that you found for me is also a member of the same church! You told me that day that God was at work in my life, and I really believe that is the truth.

I am in my seventh month of pregnancy now and going strong! I am having a daughter! She is growing fast, and as you can see from her first "picture", she is very healthy. Though we weren't so sure at one point that things were gonna come through all right.

At three months, I started bleeding. I went straight to the hospital and was told my hormone levels were very low, and "not to get my hopes up". I was put on strict bed rest and after some more tests, found out I had placenta previa. So I had to stay on bed rest.

It's a long story, but the main point is that God performed a miracle for me. The placenta previa healed itself (the doctor said that it is nothing short of a miracle). I also had a subchorionic hemorrhage. But all this time, people were praying for me. I know God listens because I have not bled in a long time, and the hemorrhage is just about gone. Thank the Lord!

I really appreciate how you helped me out in the beginning, and I very much appreciate the work you do over there at Hope. Please keep it up! I have enclosed the 4D ultrasound picture of my little angel. Can you see her face leaning on her hand? She will be here in my arms very soon.

Well, I just wanted to say thanks – and God bless you.

~Angel's Mommy

P.S.
This letter came to us in January; in March this newly married mom and dad stood on stage with their daughter and testified to our banquet guests that "there is hope" in an unplanned pregnancy.

Hope Pregnancy Centers
Broward County, Florida

THANK YOU FOR TELLING THE TRUTH

She was a college student. She was young, with a life of promise and great potential ahead. She needed a pregnancy test. She did not need a baby. She was convinced that an abortion would be her choice if the test was positive. The test *was* positive.

She was very distressed to be in conflict over a decision she thought she had already made. Reality is different from opinion. The counselor gently spoke the truth in love. It was nothing that Miss College Student **wanted** to hear; it was everything that Miss College Student **needed** to hear. Several times she said, *"Thank you for telling me the truth."* She didn't rush the counseling session; she talked a lot, and she listened for a long time. When she left, she thanked us again for telling her the truth, but said she still felt that abortion was her only option.

Later she called to say that she had decided to carry the baby. She identified friends and family who would support her decision to give life to her child. Our prayers were answered when she told us the abortion appointment had been canceled.

Our dear Miss College Student also prayed to receive Christ in the ensuing weeks...so two lives were saved! Actually, before it was all said and done, there was a young man who became a father before he had planned – and who met the Savior when he least expected it! But that is another story....

As the Center Director kept me updated on the unfolding events in this girl's life, I was grateful to God for His mercy. A child's life had been spared. That is the business we are in. Because of the decisions the parents-to-be had made, this baby would be born into a covenant household. But the *first* life that had to be saved and that

<u>God had saved</u> was the life of this young woman.

After years of talking with women who had their abortions while in college, I have heard an all-too-familiar story. Many live for *decades* following their abortions in darkness, depravity and depression because of the shame and the guilt that followed what was sold to them as a *'simple, safe procedure.'*

I know how crucial that first visit with the counselor was for Miss College Student. I know that somehow the God of the Universe intervened in this girl's life to preserve the dreams, the hopes, the potential, the possibilities, and the promises that lead to life and life abundant!

Hope Pregnancy Centers
Broward County, Florida

ABSTINENCE

"Flee from sexual immorality. All other sins a man commits are outside his body, but he who sins sexually sins against his own body."

~ I Corinthians 6:18 NIV~

HOPE FOR TOMORROW

This is a picture of our Teen Advisors, one of our most powerful weapons in the battle for life in Broward County. Because of what I see God doing in the lives of these young people, I can assure you that THERE IS HOPE FOR TOMORROW.

I want you to know that there is a core of committed Christian young people who have not bought into the lies of our culture. Instead, they have turned to God's Word for their authority and their strength.

Not only are they committed to abstinence until marriage, they have committed to abstain from the use of alcohol, drugs and tobacco during the time that they are Teen Advisors. They are committed to telling their friends "The Whole Truth" about God's plan for purity and His ability to help them keep their commitments.

I love to be in the building when these kids are here. I love to eavesdrop when they pray. I love to hear them tell the stories of encounters and conversations they have with their friends and acquaintances out there in the "real world." This is an awesome

100

group of young people who are sold out to Jesus and are wholeheartedly following His call to be salt and light in this very dark corner of the world where we live.

This program is making a HUGE difference for life! National statistics tell us that every survey that is done shows that more and more young Americans are pro-life. I am firmly convinced that abstinence programs like ours and good factual information from pregnancy care centers across our nation are at least partially responsible for this trend.

Women are choosing life for their babies; they are choosing new life in Christ for themselves – AND young people are choosing purity as a lifestyle.

Hope Pregnancy Centers
Broward County, Florida

WRONG CHOICES CAUSE PAINFUL CONSEQUENCES

The only way to really describe their posture is that they were "draped" over their chairs and desks. Many sat with arms crossed. Several glared at the young woman who stood at the front of the classroom. Some were downright rude, giggling and talking during the presentation. A few actually spoke out and challenged the truth that was being shared by the guest instructor. (*Director of our Hope for Tomorrow Program*).

As teenagers can do well, they were making it clear with every part of their beings that they were NOT interested in hearing another Abstinence Presentation. The teacher forged ahead, making every effort to ignore the raucous behavior and concentrate on the few attentive faces. All the while she prayed, "God, help me get through to them."

The second day was worse than the first, and discouragement was on the heels of the young woman who passionately wanted to share God's viewpoint of human sexuality with these young people. All of the facts and figures in the world won't convince someone whose heart is not ready to be convinced. As we all know, teenagers are invincible – just ask one, they'll tell you! After the second day she prayed again, "God, do you really want me to tell them my story? If it will reach them, I will tell them."

The third day she still wasn't sure what to do. She wasn't just teaching from the perspective of an opinion – she was teaching from the perspective of a painful experience. To that group of teenagers, this attractive young woman who stood in front of their class at the Christian school looked like she was perfect.

She talked about God and about loving Him and trusting Him and following His plan, and to those kids she sounded like she was perfect. She perceived that they were sitting in those chairs thinking, "What could you possibly know about what I'm going through?"

The lecture ended ten minutes early that day. She took a deep breath and plunged ahead. During the last ten minutes of the class, God moved. Some of the toughest kids were brought to tears as she shared her heart with them. She took them back to a time in her life when she made decisions that were outside God's will.* She shared with them the painful consequences that followed those decisions. She poured her heart out and told them it was her love and concern for each of them that compelled her to stand up in a group of hostile teenagers and tell them why they should save themselves for marriage.

Here at Hope, we never lose sight of the fact that it is HIS love that compels them – all of them. He is the one who changes hearts, who enables them to choose life, and who is the source of all hope.

Hope Pregnancy Centers
Broward County, Florida

*See Stacy's Story on page 47.

THE GIFT OF THE SECOND CHANCE

She was a college student, still living at home with her parents and had never given them any trouble. She went to church every Sunday and her mom and dad had no idea she was sexually active.

Before we gave her the pregnancy test, we talked. We talked about her relationship with her boyfriend; we talked about her plans for the future. We talked about the disappointments that her parents would feel if they knew the whole truth about her life. We talked about the differences between attending church and having a personal relationship with the living God. By her own admission, she did not know Jesus. We talked about the baby who was born in a manger at Christmastime and how He grew up to be the Savior of the world.

As this young woman and the counselor talked more, she indicated that she was unsure of her eternal destiny and wanted to be certain of her relationship to God. After the gospel was shared, she prayed and asked Jesus to forgive her sins and take control of her life. A new life was born that day! **She discovered that she served a God who specialized in second chances.**

The pregnancy test was negative, and we talked about

lifestyle changes that would keep her from having to face the fear of an unplanned pregnancy again. She understood the risks of premarital sex, and said she wanted to live a life that would be pleasing to God.

Two weeks later she returned for a retest [which was also negative], and she talked with us about some of the big decisions she was making in her life. She had broken up with the boyfriend and was developing a closer relationship with the Lord. She said she felt His spirit drawing her and knew that she wanted to grow and mature in her faith. She also shared that her relationship with her parents was improving, and that she was doing better in school, now that she could focus on her future.

Sometimes God uses us to save the life of the child in the womb. Sometimes He uses us to save the life of the child in the world.

Hope Pregnancy Centers
Broward County, Florida

NEGATIVE TEST CAN HAVE POSITIVE INFLUENCE

Did you know that approximately fifty percent of the clients who come in for a pregnancy test are not pregnant? **We thank God every time that there is a negative test! In those situations, there is no unborn child in jeopardy of losing its life, and there is a HUGE window of opportunity for us to reach this very relieved client with truth.**

Just a few weeks ago "Jessica" came in for a pregnancy test. Her fiancé had gone overseas for several months and she had gotten involved in a new relationship that had become intimate very quickly. She told the counselor that she had already made a decision to have an abortion if the pregnancy test was positive. How could she explain to her fiancé that she was having a baby that couldn't possibly be his? She was confused about the current relationship and before she even came to Hope, she had decided abortion was the best option if she were pregnant. *"That way,"* *she told us, "no one ever has to know."* Oh, how our heart breaks for these "Jessicas!"

Our well-trained counselor asked permission to share some information with her about fetal development and abortion procedures. She listened intently and asked intelligent questions along the way. She was obviously a bright young woman. As she learned about the stages of fetal growth, she exclaimed, *"How could I not know this? Why hasn't anyone ever told me this before? Shouldn't I have learned this in Science classes or something?"*

God is good and He spared her the burden of making a difficult decision that day. The test was negative, but she still had a great fear that she might be pregnant. She gladly rescheduled a follow-up visit. She left, thanking us for all of the good information we had shared with her. She was a very sweet young woman and was so appreciative of the time we had spent with her. The counselor felt an unusual tenderness for this girl. She prayed for her as the week went by. When the client leaves, we never know if they'll come back. We hoped Jessica would return.

She did come back the next week and she was relieved to have another negative test. Because of the pregnancy scare, she was very open to discussing a lifestyle change so she could avoid being in this situation again. No one had ever encouraged her to save sex for a marriage relationship. The idea seemed to fascinate her. The counselor challenged her to test the relationship she was in – to see if there was anything left when the sexual activity was taken out of the picture. Jessica left with a firm resolve to tell her boyfriend that their relationship was no longer an intimate one.

A few weeks later she stopped in just to say "Thank you!" She had broken off the relationship because she discovered that they had "nothing in common." She made a commitment to re-examine her life and think seriously about waiting until she married to resume sexual activity. And best of all, because that window of opportunity was wide open, she listened to a presentation of the Good News of Jesus Christ. She didn't make a decision that day, but she did leave saying, *"Thank you for all you have done for me. You have really given me a lot to think about."* We may never get to know how Jessica's story ends, but we are still praying for her. **Sometimes negative tests can have a very positive influence!**

Hope Pregnancy Centers
Broward County, Florida

IF ONLY

I waited. I was raised to know right from wrong and I knew you were supposed to get married before you had sex. So I waited.

I got through high school. I did a lot of things I knew you weren't supposed to do. But I made it through and graduated as a virgin.

College was a whole new world. So much freedom! So few rules! And everybody was doing it. But I waited. It was the right thing to do.

Then I fell in love. She was beautiful, she was smart, and she was everything I was looking for in the woman I wanted to spend the rest of my life with. We talked about plans for the future and living happily ever after. This was it – the relationship that you just want to give your whole self to. The waiting was over.

I will never forget the day that the frantic call came. She was so upset that I just caught pieces and bits from her conversation. Words like "pregnant" and "abortion" kept cropping up and I was so confused. I asked her to calm down and meet me at our favorite coffee shop. My mind raced as I went to meet her. A baby! I knew it was time to grow up and accept the responsibilities that were inherent with fatherhood. I had been saving money to buy a house when we got married anyway. It looked like the calendar was just going to be accelerated

By the time I got to the coffee shop, I was pretty calm. The pregnancy was unplanned, but it wasn't the end of the world. After all, we loved each other, and things would work out. Or so I thought.

We sat and talked for hours and her mind seemed closed to every possible option except abortion. I assured her of my commitment to her. I used all of the salesmanship principles that I was learning in my college business courses to sell her on the idea of marriage, security, and raising a family together. She wasn't buying. She told me she was making an appointment at a clinic near the campus and "moving on with her life." I begged her to think it over for a day or two, and we scheduled another time to meet and talk before she did anything drastic. I knew that she would see the sense in my plan when she had time to think.

I prepared carefully for that next meeting. I went to the bank and withdrew every cent I had to my name and put it in a bank bag. I made lists in my mind of all the reasons to get married and have the baby. I was ready. I approached the meeting with confidence and a certainty that everything would work out. I was already seeing myself as a dad, bouncing this new little person on my knee.

I was already seated in a booth when she came in. She slid in and took a seat across from me and the first thing I did was lay the bank bag on the table and push it towards her. "What's this?" she asked. I replied, "It is enough money for us to get married, put a down payment on a house and both stay in school. See, I told you we could work things out." I knew the physical evidence of my ability to take care of her would speak volumes. I looked into her eyes and waited for the dawning realization that everything would be all right to soften her face and put her beautiful smile back in place. I waited for something that didn't ever happen.

Her voice was controlled, quiet and firm and she did not smile as she said, "There is not enough money in the world to convince me to have this baby. I have an abortion scheduled, and there is nothing you can do to stop me. There is nothing you can say, so don't try. There is nothing you can do legally – I have checked. It is my decision, and I have made it. End of story."

A part of me died that day. I was completely and utterly devastated that this woman whom I loved was not only rejecting me – but was ending the life of my child as well. A pain entered my heart that day and now – twenty-three years later – is still a part of me. Over the years God has worked in my life to bring about healing and restoration. But the pain of regret is a pain that lasts for a lifetime. If only I had waited. If only there had been a pregnancy care center near our campus where we could have gone for help. If only – maybe those are the two saddest words in the English language.

God is faithful, and I have seen Him fulfill Isaiah 61 in my own life. He has restored the broken places. He has rewarded me with a beautiful wife and four children. He has bound up my broken heart and has allowed me to serve in a ministry position. Today I have replaced the regret of "if only" in my vocabulary with the promises of God.

~ CVM
Hope Pregnancy Centers
Broward County, Florida

Isaiah 61:1-6

The Spirit of the Sovereign LORD is on me,
because the LORD has anointed me
to preach good news to the poor.
He has sent me to bind up the brokenhearted,
to proclaim freedom for the captives
and release from darkness for the prisoners,
to proclaim the year of the LORD's favor
and the day of vengeance of our God,
to comfort all who mourn,
and provide for those who grieve in Zion--
to bestow on them a crown of beauty
instead of ashes,
the oil of gladness
instead of mourning,
and a garment of praise
instead of a spirit of despair.
They will be called oaks of righteousness,
a planting of the LORD
for the display of his splendor.
They will rebuild the ancient ruins
and restore the places long devastated;
they will renew the ruined cities
that have been devastated for generations.
Aliens will shepherd your flocks;
foreigners will work your fields and vineyards.
And you will be called priests of the LORD,
you will be named ministers of our God

THE WHOLE TRUTH

Have you noticed that we live in a world that is *in love* with the concept *of love* – while not having a clue about what *true love* really is? This February millions of dollars will be spent on greeting cards, candy, and flowers – but will we have any better grasp on *TRUE LOVE* after Valentine's Day?

The Director of Hope For Today, (our abstinence program) gave me some quotes that real kids right here in Broward County have written on their evaluation forms after hearing our presentation, *"The Whole Truth."*

I think you will be blessed by their comments, and encouraged that presenting abstinence-until-marriage is effective and realistic ~ even in today's permissive society. Given the right information and educated about God's plan for safe sex, our kids CAN make good decisions about their sexual behavior. As caring, concerned adults we have to let them know we believe in their ability to abstain!

Q: Did you learn anything NEW this week?

Answers: "That I can change my behavior and that God will forgive me, no matter what."

"That intercourse isn't the only kind of sex I need to stay away from – it's about purity."

"That having sex before marriage can kill me because of all the STDs."

"That abstinence is God's plan for me until I get married – not just for priests and nuns."

113

"That my virginity is a gift <u>from</u> God <u>to</u> me and He gave it to me so I can give it to the person I will marry."

Q: Did the presentation change your way of thinking in any way?

Answers: "Yeah, it told me that God will forgive me." "It made me sorry for some things I have already done and made me want to stop...to change my behavior, now that I know it's not too late." " That abstinence isn't all that bad, considering the consequences that I could have to deal with like pregnancy or STDs." "I am worth waiting for....I never thought about that before." "Yes, I value myself more, and I realize that my decisions not only affect me, but the people I am with AND the person I will one day marry."

Abstinence does work. It is the only way according to God's Word. We must teach it to our children.

Hope Pregnancy Centers
Broward County, Florida

PURITY REGAINED

For the past several years I have been very focused on following the directives that God put in His Word. Following Christ has changed my life for the better in every single area that I have yielded to Him. The changes are too numerous to mention.

I'm a man. I like to think of myself as a manly man. For me, that had always meant having sex with whomever I was dating. The teaching I had received was basically that the goal of any male/female relationship was to have sex. I'm ashamed now to admit that I was usually successful in achieving my goal.

After I became a Christian and started to grow in my understanding of the Scriptures, I came across some concepts that weren't too popular with me; namely the concept of purity and saving sex for the confines of a marriage relationship. Give up recreational sex? Not an easy concept for me - but I had a sincere desire to do what my Savior expected me to do - and I had a new awareness that He would help me walk in His ways.

In my life before Christ, I had many habits that led to my irresponsible behaviors. I wasn't careful about the things that passed before my eyes. I submerged myself in lots of media that increased my appetite for sex. Movies, magazines, radio, Internet pornography...all of them were readily available to me, and I wasn't at all selective about what I watched, listened to, and feasted my eyes upon.

As I read God's Word, I was so convicted that I needed to make drastic changes in this area of my life. I had elevated sensual pleasure to first place in my life. Developing Godly character was my new priority and I knew there were some action steps I had to take if I wanted to see a change.

For me, it meant canceling cable TV. It meant no more men's magazines on my coffee table. I eliminated all of the pornography from my life and even stopped going to sexually explicit movies at the theater. I turned off the radio stations that were filled with sexually suggestive content and started listening to Christian radio. I began to spend more time with Christian brothers and sisters like myself - not "perfect people", but people who had a desire for the same kind of life I now desired to have. As I began to date again, I learned that I had to even avoid kissing…the physical contact would stoke my passion and ignite desires that I could not fulfill and remain true to God's call on my life. I continued to study the Bible and to pray, asking for Divine help with my new direction.

We all have struggles. The turning point for me was when I gained the courage to share my struggles with some other Christian men. I asked them to hold me accountable. This was the beginning of real change for me. My view of women changed, and I began to see them for the valuable gift that God created them to be.

I took serious steps to change my behavior and pursued what I knew was right and good. I wanted to be able to encourage others to live according to God's principles. In order to do that, I knew I had to overcome the obstacles in my own life first.

I have found freedom from the bondage of sexual promiscuity. My sex-drive is still alive and well, but it is under control because I have changed the information that I feed my mind. Daily prayer was - and is - essential to my success in maintaining my regained purity.

Over the years I have been involved in several churches and active in many singles groups. I had accepted my singleness and was preparing myself to be a Godly husband if His plan for my future included a wife. I truly went to church to learn about Him and meet like-minded friends - I wasn't shopping for a wife!

Over time, I became very content with being single. It was then, and only then, that God brought a very special someone into my life. She wasn't the type of woman I was usually attracted to. She was very shy and quiet. I had always been attracted to extroverts like myself. But there was something different about this gentle, quiet woman. It took a long time for me to get to know her. Eventually, we went to dinner together. We talked and got to know one another. We talked about our hopes and dreams for the future…the places where life had taken us so far, and some of the triumphs and failures we had experienced in our lives.

We didn't touch, beyond a greeting kiss on the cheek. After a few months, I believed God had brought her into my life to be my wife. She felt the same way. That is when I felt it was permissible to kiss her on the lips for the first time - and even then, it was a pure, chase kiss. I didn't want to stoke those fires…I didn't want sparks flying! I wanted to preserve the wonder of this relationship and look forward to the day that we will marry.

During our courtship, we have avoided explicit and lengthy discussions about sex. We will have a lifetime together to have those discussions and to righteously fulfill the desires that they will create. We will be married in just a few days. We have been blessed in so many ways, as a result of our commitment to stay pure. The best blessing I have experienced is the emotional blessing of being obedient. It hasn't been easy. The "old" me fights with the "new" me - but the new creature in Christ that God promised I would be has emerged victorious in this area! Physically, I'm not a virgin, but spiritually I have regained my purity, just as if I had never lost it! I am entering my marriage with no guilt and no regrets.

My new wife knows what it feels like to be cherished and protected. She knows she is my friend and my confidant. When she is also my lover, it will be good and right. She will never have to wonder what our relationship is based on.

I'm so thankful that I serve a God who restores everything that the Enemy tries to take away from us. In Christ, every sin I ever committed was nailed to the cross. I know that He truly does "make all things new". He has done it for me. Am I perfect? Of course not! But with His help, I'm getting better every day, and I like the way that feels.

If you are in mourning for the purity you have lost, do not despair. Purity can be regained through a personal relationship with the Lord Jesus Christ.

~a new man
Hope Pregnancy Centers
Broward County, Florida

ABORTION

You shall not commit murder.
~ Exodus 20:13~

Moreover, you shall say to the Israelites, Any one of the Israelites, or of the strangers that sojourn in Israel, who gives any of his children to Molech [the fire god, worshiped with human sacrifices] shall surely be put to death...
~Leviticus 20:2 The Amplified Bible

TO BE OR NOT TO BE

At a medical school students were debating the eugenics of abortion. The professor presented this family history and asked the class for their opinion.

The father has syphilis. The mother has tuberculosis. They already have four children.

The first child is blind. The second has died. The third is deaf. The fourth has tuberculosis. Now the mother is pregnant again.

The professor asked: "As her doctor would you recommend an abortion?

The majority of the class decided an abortion was appropriate.

"Congratulations," said the professor. "You have just killed Ludwig Von Beethoven."

THE STORY OF TINY TIM

It was a relatively calm day in my hospital's NICU (Neonatal Intensive Care Unit). Two other nurses and I were trying to have a conversation amid the customary sounds of ventilators and heart monitors.

I was in mid-sentence when the shrill ring of the red emergency phone halted all conversation. "Come fast," the voice said urgently. "We need a neonatal nurse stat!"

Fear gripped my heart as I ran into the delivery room. Instantly, I knew the situation was critical.

"What's happening here?" I asked.

"It's an 'oops abortion,' and now it's your problem!" responded one of the nurses. For us, an "oops abortion" meant the mother's due date was miscalculated, and the fetus survived the abortion procedure.

A pediatrician was called to the scene. He ran by me with the fetus (now called a baby) in his hand and yelled in my direction, indicating he wanted me to follow him into the resuscitation room adjoining the delivery room.

I looked into the bed of the warmer as I grabbed equipment. Before my eyes was a baby boy. A very, very tiny baby boy. The doctor and I immediately made an attempt at intubation (inserting a tube down the trachea from the mouth or nose of the infant to the tip of the lungs to ventilate, expand and oxygenate them). The doctor's effort at intubation failed, which further traumatized the baby. I glanced at the doctor and hesitantly asked, "Will you attempt intubation again?"

"You've got to be kidding," he replied. "It would be inhumane to attempt to intubate this poor little thing again. This infant will never survive."

"No, Doctor, I'm not kidding," I said, "and it's my job to ask."

The doctor softened for a moment. "I'm sorry, Sharon. I'm

just angry. The mother doesn't want the inconvenience of a baby, so she comes to the hospital so she can pay somebody to get rid of it – all neat and tidy. Then the whole thing gets messed up when the fetus has the audacity to survive."

"Then everybody takes it seriously, and they call the pediatrician, who's supposed to fix it or get rid of it."

With anger in his voice, he went on, "Some lawyers will fight for the right to do whatever we want to our bodies, but watch out for what they will do when these abortions aren't so neat and tidy! A failed homicide – and oops! Then all of a sudden everybody cares, and it's turned from a 'right' into a 'liability' that someone is blamed for!"

We looked at our pathetic little patient. He was lying in the fetal position in the wrong environment, trying to get air into underdeveloped lungs that couldn't do the job. In a calmer voice, the doctor said, "Okay, Nurse, I'm going back to the office. Keep him comfortable and let me know when it's over. I'm sorry about this. Call me if you need me. I know this is a hard one. If it helps, please know it's tough for me, too."

Holding the baby's hand, I watched the doctor retreat and then glanced back at the infant before me. He was gasping for air. "Lord, help!" I prayed.

Almost instinctively, I took the baby's vitals. His temperature was dangerously low. I pushed the warmer settings as high as they could go. His heart rate was about 180-200 beats per minute. I could count the beats by watching his little chest pulsate.

I settled down a bit and began to focus on this tiny little person. He had no name, so I gave him one. Suddenly, I found myself speaking to the baby. "Tiny Tim, who are you? I am so sorry you weren't wanted. It's not your fault."

I placed my little finger in his hand, and he grasped it. As I watched him closely, I marveled that all the minute parts of a beautiful baby were present and functioning in spite of the onslaught.

I touched his toes and discovered he was ticklish! He had a long torso and long legs. I wondered if he would have become a baseball player. Perhaps he would have been a teacher or doctor.

Emotions swept over me as I thought of my friends who had been waiting and praying for years for a baby to adopt. I spoke aloud once again to the miniature baby. "They would have given you a loving and happy home. Why would people destroy you before ever considering adoption? Ignorance is not bliss, is it, Tiny Tim?"

Meanwhile, Tim put his thumb into his mouth and sucked. I hoped that gave him comfort. I continued to talk to the baby. "I'm sorry, Tim. There are people who would risk their lives for a whale or an owl before they'd even blink about what just happened to you."

Tiny Tim gasped, and his little chest heaved as if a truck were sitting on it. I took my stethoscope and listened to his tiny, pounding heart. At the moment it seemed easier to focus on physiology rather than on this baby's humanity.

He wet, and with that my mind took off again. Here was Tiny Tim with a whole set of kidneys, a bladder and connecting tubes that functioned with a very complex system of chemistry. His plumbing was all working! I turned the overhead light up and Tim turned from it, in spite of eyelids that were fused together to protect his two precious little eyes. I thought about them. They would never see a sunset, a mother's smile, or the wagging tail of a dog.

I took his temperature again. It was dropping. He was gasping for air and continued to fight for life. I stroked him gently and began to sing:

"Jesus loves the little children,
All the children of the world.
Red and yellow, black and white,
They are precious in His sight.

Jesus loves the little children of the world."

A nurse walked in. "How's the mother?" I asked.

"Oh, she's fine. She's back in her room resting. The family said they don't want to see or hear about anything. They said, 'Just take care of it.'"

The nurse retreated with one last glance at the tiny patient. "For such a little person, he's sure putting up a big fight."

I looked at Tiny Tim and wondered if he knew that what he was fighting for so hard was life – and I knew he was losing it. He was dying and his family was resting. Their words tormented me. Just take care of it! No muss and no fuss.

Then Tiny Tim moved and caught hold of my little finger. I let him hang on. I didn't want him to die without being touched and cared for. As I saw him struggle to breathe, I said, "It's okay, Tim. You can let go. You can go back to God."

His gasping started slowing down, but he still clung to my finger. I stroked the baby ever so slowly and watched him take his last breath.

"Good-bye, Tiny Tim," I whispered. "You did matter to someone."

EPILOGUE

A few years later, Sharon Dunsmore became the manager of a psychiatric unit. One day, Kathy, a young, severely depressed woman, came to see Sharon following an unsuccessful suicide attempt. As Sharon interviewed her, Kathy said she had gone through an abortion three years before, and she was having recurring nightmares. A baby was crying for help and kept calling her name.

In her dreams, Kathy searched for the baby, but she could never find him or her. As Kathy gave the name of the hospital and the names of the doctors, a disturbing realization dawned on Sharon – Kathy was Tiny Tim's mother.

Because of hospital regulations, she couldn't tell her what she knew. Time passed. Sharon was no longer a nurse or a therapist. Kathy was no longer a psychiatric patient. They ran into each other at a restaurant, where Sharon gently unfolded the story that had been hidden for so long.

Tears flowed as she gave Kathy the gift of answers. Her baby was touched and loved by a mother. He was given a name. He didn't die alone. He was sent back to a loving God.

As the visit neared an end, they held each other and wept. Sharon looked into Kathy's eyes and saw new strength and calm. There were scars, but she was beginning to heal. The nightmares were being put to rest.

Sharon still lives with the haunting impact of this experience. *A choice that was intended to be "no big deal" turned out to be a very big deal for everybody.*

Copyright by Sharon Dunsmore
PO Box 84
Smith's Creek, Mi. 48074
810-367-6091

Used by permission.

WHAT ABOUT HIS FREEDOM TO CHOOSE?

There's a lot of talk these days about "choice." The piece of information that most unmarried men are surprised by is that they don't have a choice at all regarding decisions about their unborn children.

Some time ago as I helped prepare for a women's event at my church, a young man who asked if I knew where there might be a clergyman he could talk to approached me. He was obviously very upset. After informing him that there were no men on the premises that day, I asked if I might be of assistance. He broke down and cried as he told me that he feared his girlfriend was on her way to an abortion clinic at that very moment to terminate the life of his child. He was devastated. He wanted me to tell him that we could call the police or some government agency and stop this young woman from robbing him of his role as a father.

He sobbed brokenly as he told me, "I love her, I want to marry her and be a family." Sadly, I had to tell him there was nothing he could do to stop her. When a man entrusts his seed to a woman who is not his wife, he puts his very lineage at risk. I asked permission to pray with him, and I prayed that God would intervene and somehow spare the life of that child. I gave him the phone number for our center and told him to bring her to see us, if it wasn't too late.

I don't know what ever happened to that young man or to his baby, but God used that experience that day to teach me that unplanned pregnancies can affect the men involved just as profoundly as they affect the women. The vision to have a ministry to men was born in my heart that day, and now I am being blessed by watching how God is putting the **Men of Hope** ministry together right before my very eyes!

For several years now, our post-abortion ministry to

men has focused on the needs of men who have experienced the pain of abortion. Ron Ericson is the committed volunteer who has led that study since its inception, and in March of 2002, Ron joined our staff on a part-time basis to begin the development of more comprehensive services to men.

Our vision is to have men available to talk with the partners of our female clients when they come in for a pregnancy test. We want to hold God's standard high and encourage *"the hearts of the fathers to turn toward their children."* [Malachi 4:6] We want to share the truth in love with the men, as well as with the women, and equip them to make life-affirming choices for themselves and for their children. It is a HUGE task, but we are certain that God will call out the men of His choosing to work alongside Ron in this worthy endeavor.

Poor lifestyle choices can lead to painful consequences. **Men of Hope** is focused on offering men a chance to address sexual lifestyle decisions and pregnancy challenges by offering friendship and support in the midst of crisis.

Nancy McDonald
Hope Pregnancy Centers
Broward County, Florida

HE TURNED HIS FACE TOWARD ME

I once heard someone say that if you lived near the dump long enough, you wouldn't even smell the garbage after awhile. I never lived near a dump, but I know that the saying is true because of the things that I have experienced in my own life.

Abuse was all I knew. I don't have a lot of memories of my childhood, but the ones I have are all painful. I remember seeing drawings of big, sad-eyed children and thinking, "That is what I look like. My eyes are full of sadness." My home, the place that is supposed to be a place of shelter and safety for a child, was a place where things happened to me that no child should ever have to suffer. I was a little girl, but I had no hope for the future. I couldn't even consider that there was a future for me because I was blinded by my pain and sadness.

There seemed to be an endless stream of men who were hurting my mother and me. But the confusing thing for me was the fact that my mother kept bringing them home with her. Confusion and chaos were normal for me. After awhile, it just became a way of life. I didn't even notice the smell of the garbage anymore.

As I grew into adolescence, I found ways to deal with the pain. I began to discover the escape that alcohol and drugs provided. I learned to trade sex for what I thought was love, not realizing that I was just repeating patterns of behavior that I had learned from my mother. I was really confused. My first pregnancy led me into an early marriage that ended quickly. Not knowing how to be a mother, raising a child was almost more than I could bear.

Depression marked my days, and I was medically diagnosed as schizophrenic. A very sweet man that I will call "Evan" had come into my life and tried to help me raise my son. When I became pregnant with his children, I didn't even consult him, but went and had abortions each time. He was a kind and gentle man and was heart-broken when I told him during a huge argument that I had ended several pregnancies during the time we had been together. He cried and pleaded with me to change my lifestyle and told me that he would forgive me for everything if we could just start over.

Eventually, my promiscuous behavior killed his love for me, and he was gone. He did stay in touch with me because of his genuine concern for my son. My son cried for Evan almost daily, and that added to my guilt and shame.

The next chapter of the story has a different leading man, but the facts are pretty much the same. I was caught in a trap of repeating behaviors that I had learned as a child. I lived in a fog brought about by my depression and my dependence on alcohol and drugs. I continued and continued to make bad choices and got pregnant again and again. There were too many abortions to count, but I know that there were at least fifteen. Those are the ones that God revealed to me when He began to work in my life.

The guilt and confusion over so much loss in my life built to a point where I began to have anxiety attacks. I broke out in cold sweats and vomited daily. I was falling apart and needed help. I was finally hospitalized and put in the psychiatric ward where I was promised that I would get the help I needed.

While I was in the hospital I was "grilled" daily by a group of doctors. I finally had a "breakthrough" and all of the horrible experiences of my childhood surfaced. So I talked. And I talked. And I told them about all of the ways that other people had hurt me. But I never told any of those doctors about all of the ways I had hurt myself. I never told them how ashamed I was about killing all of my babies. I never told them about the daily fear that I lived with that my little son would be taken away from me as a penalty for my many sins. That part of my life was securely locked in a file cabinet that only had one key. Somewhere deep in my soul, I knew that God was the one who had that key. The doctors sent me away with medication and a schedule of appointments for more counseling. They didn't know they sent me home with lots of secrets still haunting me. But God knew.

One of the things that I remembered during the intense counseling sessions was a recurring vision that I had throughout my childhood. In my dream, my mom and I were in the backyard, standing near the edge where the lawn met the forest behind our house. The forest was a scary place to me, and I always tried to stay near the house. But in my dream, Jesus stood at the edge of the forest and beckoned for us to come to Him. My mom and I took hold of His hands and walked with Him into a clearing and sat on a big log. The squirrels and chipmunks came and sat very near us. We laughed and played and danced around the clearing in the forest and sat within the safety of His arms. He looked at our faces, and He knew us by name. It was the only peace I had ever known – that peace I experienced in that dream. I don't know where my vision of Jesus even came from – I don't recall ever having been in church or Sunday School or having anyone tell me that there was a God who loved me. But I knew.

I will give my age away by bringing this song up, but do you remember the lyrics, "He don't love you, like I love you…if he did, he wouldn't break your heart." I started hearing that song a lot in the days following my extended hospital stay, and somehow I connected it to that vision I had as a little girl. The God of the Universe began to teach me that I had looked for love in all the wrong places, while all the time He was standing there at the edge of the forest, inviting me to come and dance with Him.

The healing didn't happen overnight. I agreed to accept His invitation to walk with Him for all of the remaining days of my life. I accepted the gift of His forgiveness for the many sins I had committed – and for all of the sins that I would ever commit for the rest of my life. I began to experience peace and joy for the first time in my life. I started to listen to His Word and to study and reflect on the deep truths hidden there. One day I heard this verse and it was the first step of a long journey back to wholeness for

130

me:

"The Lord bless you and keep you; the Lord make His face shine upon you and be gracious to you; the Lord turn His face toward you and give you peace." (Numbers 6:24-26) I knew that God had surely turned His face toward me. Now it was time for me to face myself and deal with all of the issues of grief, anger, and shame that surrounded my abortions.

After searching for just the right place to get the help I needed, I learned that the local pregnancy care centers offered a Bible study to help women deal with abortions in their past. The only problem was that I had a very difficult time *studying* anything…the years that I should have spent getting an education were wasted on alcohol, drugs, and dysfunctional behavior. I had a really hard time with reading and communicating in written form. From what I had heard, both skills were required for this class. But the Holy Spirit wouldn't let me escape, so I called and made an appointment to talk with someone.

My healing began because someone else's healing had been completed. When I met with the post-abortion group facilitator and shared my fears and inadequacies with her, she smiled and became teary-eyed. She went on to tell me that there was a woman who really wanted to help in the post-abortion ministry, but she didn't feel ready to facilitate a group session. She had already said that she would like to do a one-on-one study with someone if the need was ever present. I feel so sorry for people who don't understand how much God loves them. He had already gone to extravagant lengths to provide for my needs, even while He was preparing this other woman to minister!

I thank God every day for the pregnancy centers that understand the huge need for post-abortion ministry. It wasn't easy to look back down the dark corridor of my life and face the things I had done. But I did it. He gave me strength – and He gave me a woman who truly had compassion for me, because she had also experienced the pain that comes from abortion.

The hardest – and most rewarding – thing of all was understanding that my babies are secure with God the Father for all eternity, and that because of my relationship with Him, I will meet them one day in Heaven. A lot of people get kind of squeamish when they hear that the people in post-abortion groups name the babies that they lost to abortion. They get real nervous when you tell them that God supernaturally reveals the identity of your child to you. But He does. He did it for me fifteen times.

Because of what Jesus did for me, I don't suffer anymore. I can more clearly understand what I was doing when I chose abortion again and again as an answer to my pregnancies, and how it was all connected to the abuse in my childhood, and the poor choices I continued to make throughout most of my adult life. The title of the Bible study is "Forgiven and Set Free", and thanks to the grace of God and Hope Pregnancy Center, now I am forgiven and set free.

As a memorial for my children, I want to share with you their names and the verses that God spoke to me as He shared their identities with me. Do not be overwhelmed with grief as I personalize my losses…remember that I will hold them in Heaven forever. For now, I hold them in my heart.

~ a forgiven woman
Hope Pregnancy Centers
Broward County, Florida

Moses (Hebrew) 'taken from the water'
"He has made everything beautiful in its time. He has also set eternity in the hearts of men; yet they cannot fathom what God has done from beginning to end." ~ Eccl . 3:11

Yolanda (Greek) 'violet flower
"For with you is the fountain of life; in your light we see light." ~ Psalm 36:9

Rosita (Greek) 'rose'
"The desert and the parched land will be glad; the wilderness will rejoice and blossom." ~ Isaiah 35:1

Francesca (French) 'free one'
"Before they call I will answer; while they are still speaking, I will hear." ~ Isaiah 65:24

Sara (Hebrew) 'princess/one who laughed'
"All glorious is the princess in her chamber; her gown is interwoven with gold." ~ Psalm 45:13

Abel (Hebrew) 'breath'
"And live a life of love, just as Christ loved us and gave himself up for us as a fragrant offering and sacrifice to God."
~ Ephesians 5:2

Bobby (English-Robert) 'bright, shining with fame'
"We know that we live in Him and He in us because He has given us of His Spirit." ~ I John 4:13

Esmeralda (Spanish) 'adorned one'
"Do not be afraid, little flock, for your father has been pleased to give you the kingdom." ~ Luke 12:32

Anastasia (Greek) 'of the resurrection'
"And if the Spirit of Him who raised Jesus from the dead is living in you, He who raised Christ from the dead will also give life to your mortal bodies through His Spirit, who lives in you." ~ Romans 8:11

Anastasios (Greek) 'resurrected one'
"And if the Spirit of Him who raised Jesus from the dead is living in you, He who raised Christ from the dead will also give life to

your mortal bodies through His Spirit, who lives in you."
~ Romans 8:11

Ruth (Hebrew) 'compassionate, beautiful'
"Your hands made me and formed me, give me understanding to learn your commands." ~ Psalm 119:73

Nicolas (Greek) 'victorious army'
"But thanks be to God! He gives us the victory through our Lord Jesus Christ." ~ I Corinthians 15:57

Christina (French) 'beautiful Christian'
"For we do not preach ourselves, but Jesus Christ as Lord, and ourselves as your servants for Jesus' sake."
~ 2 Corinthians 4:5

Nyhim (Middle Eastern – Nadim) 'friend of God'
"I tell you, whoever acknowledges me before men, the son of Man will also acknowledge him before the angels of God." ~ Luke 12:8

Nicodemus (Greek-Nico) 'the Lord lives'
"The Lord lives! Praise be to my Rock! Exalted be God my Savior!" ~ Psalm 18:46

Matthew (Hebrew) 'gift of Jehovah'
"The Lord makes His face shine upon you and be gracious to you." ~ Numbers 6:25

"I have redeemed you; I have called you by name, you are mine." ~ Isaiah 43:1

SOMETIMES YOU JUST NEED TO GET ANOTHER PERSPECTIVE

A very brave woman shared her testimony about her own two abortions at a recent volunteer training seminar. I noticed the cute blond girl on the front row crying quietly throughout the testimony. That isn't so unusual…often hearing another person share the pain of their past abortion will evoke painful memories for those who are listening.

I wasn't surprised when she asked to speak with me privately after class. I mentally prepared my "abortion isn't the unforgivable sin" speech and planned to direct her to enroll in our post-abortion class. **But I was surprised** when she stood in my office with clenched fists and cried out angrily, "I'm really having a hard time with this! How could ANYONE do that – especially someone who already had children?"

It took me a minute to realize that **she** was not post abortive and that she was actually angry at the person who had been so vulnerable and shared her testimony with the group of trainees.

This was new territory for me…I breathed a quick prayer and asked God for words to speak. The thoughts that I shared with

135

this young woman were about trying to understand things from another person's perspective.

Though it sounded trite, the old Indian adage about not criticizing someone until you have walked in his/her moccasins was really the essence of what I shared with her – as well as the biblical admonition to "judge not, lest you be judged."

Abortion IS a terrible thing – we see the havoc and devastation that it wreaks in the lives of the women and men who choose it; we see the horrific loss of life of innocent unborn children, and we know that it grieves our Creator who made life to be a sacred trust.

But we are under a high command from our Heavenly Father to "love one another." We don't have to do **anything** except love them the way Jesus would love them...**with all our hearts.** When we do that, He allows us the joy of seeing what He can do to soften a heart, to change a life, and to broaden our perspective. That is the reason we always say, "There is hope – because **with** God's grace, all things are possible." How could ANYONE do such a horrible thing? Because **without** God's grace, **all** of us could do horrible things.

The cute blond is now a volunteer at one of our centers. God gave her His perspective and she is ministering to the women He sends her way. She has a new appreciation of the fact that He loved her enough to spare her from having to ever face a decision about abortion.

She has a new perspective and a tender heart toward the women who have experienced the pain of abortion. She offers hope and help to those who are in the midst of making decisions about life and eternal life. *Sometimes you just need to get another perspective!*

Hope Pregnancy Centers
Broward County, Florida

Abortion Breaks the Heart of God
It Breaks Our Hearts As Well

See the woman on the sidewalk,
See the pain within her eyes.
Deceived by those who said they cared, but gave her naught but
lies.
They said it was a simple choice,
And though she heard that still small voice...
She turned her back, was deafened by the sound of Satan's cries.

And now it seems that all is black and hopeless, dark and cold.
Her arms are empty at her side, she has no child to hold.
Oh, why did no one tell her of the pain she'd have to bear?
Is there no one who will understand, reach out to her and care?

The Lord in His compassion reaches deep into her soul,
"Turn to me my child" He whispers, "I will make you whole.
I sent my Son to die for you that you might be set free.
I've waited long to see the day when you would come to me."

J.H.
        a survivor of abortion – now forgiven and set free

Psalm 32:1-5

"What happiness for those whose guilt has been forgiven! What joys when sins are covered over! What relief for those who have confessed their sins and God has cleared their record! There was a time when I wouldn't admit what a sinner I was. But my dishonesty made me miserable and filled my days with frustration. All day and all night Your hand was heavy upon me. My strength evaporated like water on a sunny day until I finally admitted all my sins to You and stopped trying to hide them. I said to myself, 'I will confess my sins to the Lord.' And you forgave me! All my guilt is gone!"

Hope Pregnancy Centers
Broward County, Florida

Strength and Power

When a person can come to the place in life where they can say with absolute unwavering conviction, "Yes, but my God is in control," there is an awesome sense of strength and assurance that will fill the heart to overflow with an indescribable joy and peace. No matter what the challenges we face in life, this peace can remain.

By Charles Stanley
From his book *God Is In Control*

STORIES OF HOPE

"But the Eyes of the Lord are on those who fear him,
On those whose hope is in His unfailing love,
To deliver them from death and
Keep them alive in famine."

~Psalms 33:18-19 NIV~

I HAD NO IDEA

I'm a grandfather who has a home-based business. I wasn't looking for a job in a pregnancy care center – or anywhere else for that matter! My wife and I got involved in a new church start-up in an urban neighborhood, and I figured that was enough work for me.

Then our pastor started talking about the needs of women in our neighborhood for the services of a pregnancy center. All of us knew that there was a section very near our church where the prostitutes solicited for business. The pastor said that a local ministry had approached us and asked if we would be interested in partnering with them to offer hope and help to our community. This partnership idea was new in pregnancy care center ministry and we would be a perfect test case. Our church decided to give space for this group to come in and offer their free and confidential services to the women in our community. I still didn't see how this new partnership would affect me in any way. After all, I'm a grandfather who owns his own business, remember?

Then the lady from the pregnancy center came to speak to the church and challenged us to see this work as a missions opportunity. She suggested that God might even call people from our church to get involved and help. I still didn't feel like there was any connection to me. What could a grandfather do to help women in unplanned pregnancies? As she finished the presentation, she added one more thought, "…and if there is a man here who has flexibility with his business during the hours that we are here, it would be wonderful to have security – all of us know that this neighborhood can be dangerous. It would really help the ladies to feel safe if we could just have a man present."

I decided to check this ministry out – to find out for myself what it was all about. I learned a lot that first day I showed up to be a security guard and at the end of the day, I couldn't think of any reason that would not allow me to give them four hours of my time each week. "Why not?" was what I said to myself.

I showed up at 9:30 AM that first morning the center opened and helped put up signs, move furniture and organize things. After all the preparation was done, we formed a prayer circle, and each of us prayed for God to send the clients in. As I recall, no one showed up on that first day, so there was plenty of time to talk to the staff members and other volunteers who were there to serve. I gained an even deeper understanding of the mission of the pregnancy care center ministry and was completely convinced that I should be there to help whenever possible.

One of the things that grandfathers love to do is watch their grandchildren "perform." I'm sure my five year old grandson is a future major league soccer player, so when my daughter called one Friday afternoon and asked if I could give her a ride to the soccer game the next morning, I was glad to say yes. Watching my little guy and his team- mates play soccer is like watching a swarm of bees looking for a new hive. It is hilarious, and I can't think of anything I would rather do.

As we drove to the soccer field the next morning, we made the typical small talk – "How was your week?" – "Fine, how was yours?" etc. As we waited for the game to start, Roseanne asked absent-mindedly, "So, Dad, what's new with you?" I was so excited about my new role as a volunteer at the pregnancy center that I began to tell her about it. She didn't really respond, but amidst all of the chaos of the soccer field, I didn't think much about it.

Later, during a break in the game, she turned to me and laid her hand on my arm. "Dad," she began with a big breath, "I just want to tell you something. Hope Pregnancy Centers is the reason your grandson is here!" I was speechless, trying to figure out what in the world she was talking about.

143

She went on to fill in the details…the pregnancy came at a bad time in her life. My wife and I were living in another state at the time. We talked to her frequently by phone and believed that she was doing well. But she did not seek advice from us when she decided to have an abortion. Roseanne called a friend and asked if she would go to the abortion clinic with her and drive her home afterwards. The girlfriend agreed – under one condition – Roseanne had to agree to go to the pregnancy center first and speak with a counselor. Roseanne agreed to appease her friend and they scheduled an appointment.

Roseanne told me that they talked to her about the methods that were used to do abortions. "Dad, I had no idea that the baby was so perfectly formed at such an early stage," she told me. She said the counselor talked to her about God and asked permission to share some verses from the Bible with her. Roseanne prayed to receive Christ that day and decided to carry her baby. Thanks to God's unfailing love and to the obedient servants at Hope Pregnancy Centers, I have a five-year-old little grandson today who sits on my lap and calls me "Grandpa." I had no idea that his life was ever in jeopardy.

It is hard for me to hold back the tears when I see how God has woven all of the pieces in this story together in His perfect timing. Why would a grandfather get involved and help out at a pregnancy care center? I thought it was a good thing to do…I had no idea how God had already used this ministry to bless me. And I am convinced that I have no idea about the many, many ways He will use it to bless me in future days.

~ Grandpa Ray
Hope Pregnancy Centers
Broward County, Florida

144

The Friendship Factor

I have been involved with pregnancy center ministry for many years – first as a steering committee member, helping start a brand new ministry, then as a board member for ten years, as the Director of Development (a paid staff position) for eighteen months, and for the last several years as the Executive Director.

Our basic message is that we help young women in unplanned pregnancies and provide *friendship and support* for them during a difficult time in their lives. I have had many occasions over the last fifteen plus years to tell people how we help these young women choose life for their babies and new life in Christ for themselves. Many times as I have made presentations in churches, I have said, *"Unplanned pregnancy happens…it is no respecter of persons, it happens in good, upstanding Christian families, and it happens to people whom we know and love."*

Last summer 'unplanned pregnancy' visited my own family, and those words became a painful reality in my life. *My daughter was pregnant* - how could this happen? I cried out to God and said, "You know, it doesn't look so good for you – or for the ministry - when the Executive Director's daughter gets pregnant…how can this situation ever be used to glorify Your name?"

I went to my board of directors and offered to resign. They were exemplary in their grace and support during a difficult season. Many shared their own stories with me of disappointments and challenges in their families. They reminded me that it wasn't my business to make decisions for my adult children. God protects His own name and reputation!

My life verse – and our key verse here in our ministry is Jeremiah 29:11. It says, *"For I know the plans I have for you,"* declares the Lord, *"plans to prosper you and not to harm you; plans to give you a hope and a future."*

145

Last summer I gained a new understanding of the meaning of that verse as we talked with our daughter about the options that were open for her. She and her boyfriend chose to marry and parent their baby. In the midst of an unplanned pregnancy, we had to trust God that they made a good choice; that is part of His plan to give them a hope and a future.

There was a small, quiet, end-of-summer wedding, and the most beautiful little baby girl in the world was born in January, granting me entrance into the wonderful world of being "Grandma"! *How can such a blessing come out of such a painful circumstance?* I didn't realize that I was holding onto a great deal of anger at my daughter until that baby was born, and I felt it all melt away. The past is past, and God has given new life, and life is a precious gift.

I didn't want to learn about unplanned pregnancy this way. But God's ways are not our ways, and I am already seeing His hand at work, teaching me lessons about this ministry that I could not have learned any other way.

The *friendship factor* is one of the most powerful lessons that He has impressed upon me. When I think back on the special times I have shared with *friends* in my life, I know that the influence of caring friends has made me a better person. Since I was a little girl, it was my girlfriends I turned to for inspiration, for recreation and for consolation. We have shopped together, eaten together, traveled together, laughed together, cried together, prayed together, shared our sorrows and our joys – and commiserated over unappreciative husbands, rebellious children, non-cooperative business associates, and various other issues of secular and spiritual concern!

Friendships have helped me live up to promises I have made. They have helped me say no to things I shouldn't be part of and have given me reason to know I am loved and appreciated on those days when I just want to have a pity party.

Seasons of our lives come and go – we move away, we

gain new interests, and paths that were once so closely on a parallel course diverge in different directions – but I know that one hour over a cup of coffee will catch us up and we'll be able to pick up where we left off – that's the kind of friendships I have been blessed with in my life.

As I helped my daughter shop for maternity clothes and furnish the nursery and gather the newborn layette for the baby, I was struck by the fact that, in the midst of the crisis, *I was her only friend*.

Our relationship has become closer than it ever was before because I have become her friend, as well as her mother. That is when the neon lights started to flash in my brain and I knew there was a message in all of this that related to my ministry here at the pregnancy care center. If my twenty-one-year-old daughter didn't have friends who were mature enough to stand beside her through the unplanned pregnancy, then there are other young women who face unplanned pregnancies alone, too!

My daughter was blessed to be in a relationship with a young man who accepted the responsibility of fatherhood and wanted to marry her and be a family. Many of our clients have absolutely no support of any kind; they are deserted by the men who claim to love them; they are pressured to abort by family members and people who call themselves friends…they are often afraid and truly alone. *I have resolved that we must be more aggressive in offering friendship to our community through the outreach of our pregnancy care center ministry!*

The girls who come to us looking for hope just need a friend to encourage them, to talk to them, to tell them the truth in love, and to stand beside them. It is our desire as a ministry to be that friend and provide support for them that will enable them to make life-affirming decisions.

If they had a mom or an aunt or a friend who was able to help them, they wouldn't be coming to us for basic needs like maternity clothes and baby items! Offering friendship and support in Jesus' name is the only way we can show young women in unplanned pregnancies that "there is hope."

It is the human condition to ask, "Why me, God?" and that was my initial reaction to the news that my daughter was pregnant. He answered me very clearly, "Why not you? Aren't you the one who claims to know how to respond to the unplanned pregnancy? Show me that you really mean it."

~ an Executive Director

DON'T WORRY, BABE, I'LL TAKE CARE OF EVERYTHING

"He told me he would love me forever. When I told him I was pregnant, he held me close and said, 'Don't worry, babe, I'll take care of everything.'

I thought he meant he would marry me and we would have the baby. He meant he would pay for an abortion."

At Hope Pregnancy Centers, we specialize in mending broken hearts. You would think that February would be a time of celebrating love for a lifetime and special relationships. The greeting card companies certainly promote the love messages on all those Valentines! But like Miranda whose words appear in quotes at the top of this story, all too many young women have learned that what they thought was a love that would last forever, quickly turned into a relationship that left them with hurts, disappointments, a broken heart – and sometimes, a baby on the way.

Miranda and her boyfriend hadn't really talked about the future. Their relationship had started out as 'just good friends', had progressed to a dating relationship after several weeks, and then became intimate. Miranda told the counselor, "I don't even remember talking about moving to the next level...we were just kissing on the couch one night when my parents were out of town and the next thing I knew, clothes were gone, and things were out of control. I cried afterwards. He said he was sorry and that it wouldn't happen again. The only thing I remember is waking up the next morning and thinking, 'I'm not a virgin anymore.' After that, making love just became a routine part of our relationship. It wasn't so special because we had to sneak around and make sure our parents didn't know – and there was always the fear of getting pregnant. At first, we talked about getting married after we finished college – but after a few months we didn't really talk about the future anymore."

Miranda's heart was broken because the man she gave herself to turned out to be unworthy of her love and trust. He offered to pay for an abortion, but that was all he offered to do to "help." At the time of this writing, Miranda still isn't sure if she will parent her baby or place for adoption, but she has no intention of having an abortion. Her heart is broken, her boyfriend is gone, and she is facing difficult decisions in the days ahead.

We need to be here to assure girls like Miranda that there is a faithful God who has a wonderful plan for each life; plans to give each one of us a hope and a future. Boyfriends don't always keep their promises, but we serve a God who is a covenant keeper and His promises last forever!

"Know therefore that the LORD your God is God; He is the faithful God, keeping His covenant of love to a thousand generations of those who love Him and keep His commands." Deuteronomy 7:9-10

Hope Pregnancy Centers
Broward County, Florida

150

A DAY IN THE LIFE OF A PREGNANCY CENTER

I know that your life is probably like mine – there are those mountaintop experiences when we feel invincible, when we see God work with His mighty power, the times we just want to sing and shout His praises. Here at the pregnancy center we experience that same thing as an organization...there are times when He just shows up in a dramatic way and does His thing. **Then Monday comes.**

The phone rings. **"Do you give out the Morning After Pill?"**

"No, we are not a medical clinic – but do you know for sure that you are pregnant?"

"Yes – I'm about four weeks pregnant. I'm married, but only for about a year. We're not ready to have a baby."

"Well, you have called the right place. We can help you explore all of your options. We have good, accurate information and we can offer you a free test that is 99.9% accurate, according to the manufacturer. Could I make an appointment for you to visit one of our centers? All of our services are free and confidential."

"No, thank you." She hangs up. The staff and volunteers gather and pray that God will speak to her heart.

The phone rings again. **"I just found out my 15 year old daughter's best friend is pregnant. I got your name from our youth pastor. He said you could help."**

"Yes, we can. If you will give her our number and encourage her to call us, we will schedule an appointment for her to come in and talk to one of our counselors."

"Will you do the abortion on the same day she comes in?" (Oh, no! She thinks we are an abortion clinic!)

"We do not provide abortions, but we have good, accurate

151

information that will help her know about all of the options available to her. All of our services are free and confidential so she doesn't have to worry about the cost. "

"This girl has no business having a baby – she is just a child herself. Can you refer us to someone who provides abortions?"

"We do not provide referrals for abortion either – our experience tells us that abortion is a permanent solution to a problem that is only temporary."

"Well, she really needs to make a decision and get on with her life."

"I'm so glad that you realize it is _her_ decision. As her friend, I encourage you to help her gather enough information about alternatives to abortion to make an informed decision. Whatever she chooses, she will have to live with her decision for the rest of her life. Please encourage her to call us before she makes a final decision."

"Thanks." She hangs up. The staff and volunteers gather and pray that God will speak to the heart of this "would-be helper" and also to the heart of the pregnant teenager.

These are two real phone calls – calls that I answered myself on the Monday morning after our banquet. They came to our administrative office before business hours. Can you imagine the many, many calls like these that come to centers all over America every day?

Gifts from the private sector allow us to be here to answer the phones with compassion, with truth, and with the words that we have been trained to use to encourage life choices. Remember that _the resurrected Jesus is our hope_. He uses ordinary people to help offer that hope to women and men in unplanned pregnancies.

Hope Pregnancy Centers
Broward County, Florida

152

MEN OF HOPE
We are challenging them to be like Joseph

Recently someone snickered when I told them that our mission statement was helping women **and men** in unplanned pregnancies. The laughter gave evidence to our society's erroneous viewpoint that an unplanned pregnancy is a woman's issue. The last biology class I attended taught me that it takes a female and a male to create a pregnancy – planned or otherwise!

As I began to write a letter for the December newsletter, I was tempted to write about Mary's unplanned pregnancy, which miraculously resulted in her giving birth to the Savior of the World. But as I thought about the familiar story of Christmas, I got stuck on Joseph.

In recent years, we have developed an increased awareness of the crucial impact that the men in their lives have on our clients. As I searched the Scripture for the few verses that are written about Joseph, the earthly father who raised Jesus, <u>I was struck by the fact that we are encouraging our male clients to be like Joseph!</u>

Joseph was frightened and confused. But if you look at the few verses recorded about Joseph in Matthew (1:20, 1:24, 2:13, 2:14, 2:29, 2:21) and in Luke (2:4, 2:22, 2:48), you will discover the supernatural ways that God spoke to Joseph and instructed him.

You will see that Joseph was quick to carry out the instructions that he was given. You will understand that he was a man who loved his wife, loved his family, was a concerned father, and had a deep desire to do the right thing – even when he knew that people around him wouldn't understand.

The young men who come to the pregnancy center are frightened and confused, too. We have an awesome program called Men of Hope. For many years, we have been leading men to discover hope for healing and restoration in the aftermath of abortion through a Bible study entitled "Healing A Father's Heart."

More recently, we have been training male counselors to minister to the fathers of our clients' babies. These dedicated, godly men take the time to listen to the fears and concerns that these young men have about fatherhood. Many of them have never had a father figure in their own lives. It is little wonder that they don't know the right thing to do.

Our counselors encourage them to confront facts. They share information with them about fetal development and the risks of abortion. They advise them that not only does an abortion have long-term negative psychological effects on women, but on men as well. All in all, these men do encourage the would-be fathers to be like Joseph.

They assure them that there is a God who loves them and has a wonderful plan for their life. They tell them that He will supernaturally equip them to make good decisions and to learn to be good fathers. They encourage these young men, according to Malachi 4:5-6, *"See, I will send you the prophet Elijah before that great and dreadful day of the LORD comes. He will turn the hearts of the fathers to their children, and the hearts of the children to their fathers; or else I will come and strike the land with a curse."* (NIV)

Hope Pregnancy Centers
Broward County, Florida

DIVINE APPOINTMENT

"I have considered my ways and have turned my steps to your statues. I will hasten and not delay to obey your commands."
~Psalms 119:59-60 NIV

Sometimes, the words "unplanned pregnancy" just don't fit. It is not unusual for us to meet unmarried clients who have gotten pregnant on purpose. From our perspective it may look like an "unwise" pregnancy or even a "crisis" pregnancy, but when these young people come to us for help, we have a duty to see it as a Divine appointment. We look for ways to share the love of Christ with them.

Jane and Ozzie were seventeen years old when they came to us. They were pretty sure that the pregnancy test would be positive – and they were excited about that. They were in love, and they planned to marry someday. They didn't seem overly concerned that the arrival of the baby and the timing of the wedding might be in reverse order.

We could have preached. We could have pressured them to rush into marriage before the baby's birth. We could have capitalized on Jane's profession of faith in Christ and imposed a good dose of guilt. We could have done a lot of things that would *not* have helped them know the love of Jesus Christ. So we listened. And we prayed. And we recognized that even this "wanted" baby was not out of jeopardy until he actually entered the world.

In the pregnancy care center we have lots of terminology that we use every day...like *"unplanned pregnancy"; "abortion-vulnerable"; "abortion-minded"; "biological father"; "supportive father"*...and on and on. According to Jane and Ozzie, this was not an unplanned pregnancy. But if his parents weren't willing to provide a place for them to live, would they

155

have been *"abortion-minded"*? If Ozzie didn't have a job to provide an income to help his family, would they have been *"abortion-vulnerable"*?

It all comes down to the "any given day" factor. *Any* woman can be at-risk for abortion on any given day. Everyone who walks in the door of a pregnancy center is treated as a Divine appointment. It all comes down to that face-to-face encounter when our counselors fall in love with the clients. Our counselor fell in love with Jane and Ozzie when they came to our center. She was able to see them through the eyes of Jesus. She talked to them about His wonderful plan for their lives. She rejoiced with them when the baby was born.

Jane is certain that she has a personal relationship with Christ; Ozzie has listened to our counselor share the truth, but isn't sure about making a commitment just yet. The only thing he is certain about is that he loves Jane and he loves their baby. **That's a start!** Pray for them to turn their steps to His statues.

Hope Pregnancy Centers
Broward County, Florida

156

TIME CHANGES THINGS

Isn't it amazing how time changes things? The whole concept of time is something that is incomprehensible to the human mind. In Scripture the word "time" is used 770 times! The concept of eternity is mentioned 85 times! Ecclesiastes 3:11 even tells us that in our human state we don't understand time: *"He (God) has made everything beautiful in its time. He has also set eternity in the hearts of men; yet they cannot fathom what God has done from beginning to end."*

Last year a young married couple, not knowing who we were, came to us looking for an abortion. They were tense, they were nervous, and there was no joy evident in their demeanor. They thought they were pregnant and, in their opinion, the timing was all wrong. We sat with them and shared the truth in love. We talked about life beginning at conception. We talked about the fact that God has a perfect plan for every life. The pregnancy test was negative. It wasn't time for them to be parents, but it was time for them to reflect on their outlook on life and their dependence on God.

Times marches on...not long ago this same couple came in for a pregnancy test. This time they were obviously excited about the possibility of a baby in their home. The positive pregnancy test brought smiles and tears of joy! They came back to a place called Hope...they knew we would rejoice with them. Time can change our responses...but only God can change our hearts. He truly does make all things beautiful in His time.

Hope Pregnancy Centers
Broward County, Florida

HOPE

Luke 7:37-50 NIV

"When a woman who had lived a sinful life in that town learned that Jesus was eating at the Pharisee's house, she brought an alabaster box of perfume, and as she stood behind him at his feet, weeping, she began to wet his feet with her tears. Then she wiped them with her hair, kissed them and poured perfume on them.

When the Pharisee who had invited him saw this, he said to himself, ' If this man were a prophet, he would know who is touching him and what kind of woman she is – that she is s sinner.'

Jesus answered him, 'Simon, I have something to tell you.'

'Tell me, teacher,' he said.

'Two men owed money to a certain moneylender. One owed him five hundred denarii, and the other fifty. Neither of them had the money to pay him back, so he canceled the debts of both. Now which of them will love him more?'

Simon replied, 'I suppose the one who had the bigger debt canceled.'

'You have judged correctly,' Jesus said.

Then he turned toward the woman and said to Simon, 'Do you see this woman? I came into your house. You did not give me any water for my feet, but she wet my feet with her tears and wiped them with her hair. ... You did not put oil on my head, but she has poured perfume on my feet. Therefore, I tell you, her many sins have been forgiven – for she loved much. But he who has been forgiven little loves little.'

Then Jesus said to her, 'Your sins are forgiven.'

The other guests began to say among themselves, 'Who is this who even forgives sins?'

Jesus said, 'Your faith has saved you; go in peace.'"

Sharp, professional, business owner, and a single mom...all those words describe her today – those words and much more.

But that is not who she was the first time she came to the pregnancy center. At that time she was living on the street. She was addicted and desperate. Prostituting herself to support her habit, she was a victim of her own past and the series of bad choices she had made. She was a lost cause if ever there was one.

How could a story like that get any worse? She was pregnant. She simply could not, should not, have this baby. A friend brought her to our door because her name was Hope – *and so was ours*.

Fortunately, we do not counsel from our own wisdom and experience. We are bound to a God who offers hope. We are prisoners of hope and cannot run from that truth even when it seems that hope is lost or surely misplaced. This "Hope" was surely lost AND misplaced, but God gave us the gift of being part of His plan for her life. Unseen realities and whispered potentials all live within our walls and reside within our spirits. There is a God who assures us of that hope, which is found in Christ alone.

We did not believe that this woman could "pull herself up by her bootstraps." We did not think that we could deliver her from her circumstance. We did not even "hope" that everything would turn out okay. We put our hope in Christ Jesus alone and in His redemption, His power, and His Word.

Jesus gave us many examples in the New Testament of meeting the present need. One such example is found in the scripture preceding this story. The woman in that story had sinned much, and she was forgiven much.

We knew our client had a very present need to escape the lifestyle she was living. After much discussion and many, many phone calls, she left the area to go to a drug treatment center, and we prayed for God to protect the child she carried, not knowing if we would ever see her again.

Months later she came in – clean, sober, and beautifully

pregnant! God had done an amazing work in her life. He had prepared her heart to take in the truth of His unconditional love for her. She invited Christ to take control of her life and has been growing in her commitment to Him ever since that day. He calmed her fears and proved His faithfulness to her by giving her a beautiful, healthy baby girl. As a testimony to her new understanding of His love for her, she named the baby Grace.

Hope and Grace – that sums up what happens in the pregnancy center better than anything else we could say. He IS a God of unlimited hope, and He is the one who gives us the grace to understand and receive that truth.

Because of that, the description in the first paragraph of this story describes who this woman is today! If you met her, you would never connect her to the client who first visited us on that long ago day.

Now she writes articulate thank you notes to us and puts Scripture references at the bottom of the card! She makes Christmas gifts for us, bakes homemade cookies, and speaks to ladies' group on our behalf.

She is growing in her knowledge of God's Word, and she is implementing it in every area of her life. Hope and Grace are two of our most dedicated Walkers for our annual Walk For Life Event! Now the one who came to us needing a blessing IS a blessing to our whole ministry!

The phone will ring again at any moment. It will be a young woman who is lost and afraid. She may be addicted and living on the street. She will fear that she might be pregnant and will wonder if we can help.

We will tell her to "COME ON IN!" This is a place of hope and grace.

Hope Pregnancy Centers
Broward County, Florida

160

I WANT TO GROW UP

Grace wants to grow up. In the previous story, you read about a client named Hope. God rescued her from, in her words, a "very ugly life" and brought her to one of our centers. Over a period of several months, He allowed us to minister to her. She accepted Christ as her Savior and chose life for her baby. Grace is three years old now and I am blessed to enjoy the company of both of these special ladies frequently. Just the other day we traveled together to talk to a ladies Bible Study group at one of our local churches. As Hope and I chatted, Grace called from the backseat, "Mommy!" When her mommy said, "Yes, Grace...what do you want?" This delightful child replied, "I want to grow up."

Grace is growing up. She is growing in the nurture and admonition of the Lord because her mommy chose life AND new life in Christ over three years ago. When we train new volunteers, we remind them over and over again that our ministry is woman-focused, not baby-focused. That day in the car with Hope and Grace I was reminded anew that it isn't about the baby. It is about sharing Jesus with the hurting women who walk through our doors. It is about trusting Him with the details of "very ugly lives". It is about little girls who grow up, loved by mommies who love Jesus. There is hope for the future because we serve a God who is all about hope and grace.

Monday morning comes every week. Today I answered the phone and a woman asked, "Do you use general anesthetic when you do the abortions? I don't want it to hurt." In the few seconds before I began to speak, I prayed. (*Lord, touch her heart; help her listen.*) There was no way I could tell her that there is not enough anesthetic in the world to numb the pain that abortion causes. I have been hearing the stories of the wounded women and men for all of the fifteen years I have been involved in this ministry.

"We are not a medical clinic, but we do have some good information about abortion. Do you know for sure that you are pregnant?" Our goal is to attempt to engage these abortion-minded women in conversation so that we might have an opportunity to show concern and compassion for them, even over the telephone. When we tell them that all of our services are free, some will make an appointment and come in to talk. We never mislead them, always making sure that they know we do not provide abortions or referrals for abortion.

Asking good questions in a non-judgmental way is one way that we attempt to build a relationship in the few seconds/minutes that we have her on the phone. My Monday morning phone call wasn't interested in anything except an abortion. (*God, are you listening to my prayers?*) "Do you know what kind of abortion you would need?" I asked, in one last effort to keep her on the line. "Yes, I need one where they use general

162

anesthetic because I don't want to feel the pain." The line went dead and I cried for the child who may not get to grow up. (*Lord, did you touch her heart? Will you save her? What about the baby she carries? Your will be done on earth as it is in Heaven. Amen.*)

We will still be here to help pick up the pieces when they come back to us "after the choice", when the pain is too difficult to bear.

Hope Pregnancy Centers
Broward County, Florida

IT'S NO ACCIDENT THAT I AM HERE

"Jesus answered her, "If you knew the gift of God and who it is that asks you for a drink, you would have asked Him and He would have given you living water." "Sir, the woman said, "you have nothing to draw with and the well is deep. Where can you get this living water? Are you greater than our father Jacob, who gave us the well and drank from it himself, as did his sons and his flocks and herds?" Jesus answered, "Everyone who drinks this water will be thirsty again, but whoever drinks the water I give him will never thirst. Indeed, the water I give him will become in him a spring of water welling up to eternal life."
John 4:10-14 NIV

The woman who met Jesus at the well on that hot, dusty afternoon was there to draw water. During that brief encounter, she got a lot more than she bargained for! She came to the well, broken and guilty – she left that day with joy in her heart. That is often what happens with the women who come through the doors at pregnancy centers all across the country. Let me tell you about one of them…

Natalie came to us, hoping her pregnancy test would be negative. She was already a single parent and knew first-hand how difficult it was to raise a child by herself. She was dismayed to think that she might be pregnant again.

As the counselor talked with Natalie, she discovered that church attendance had been a part of Natalie's childhood. She told the counselor "I know my mother has prayed for me to come to know the Lord for a very long time." She went on to say that she wasn't ready to do that until she "knew it was for real" – she didn't want to cave in to the pressure from her mom, she didn't want to "use God as a crutch", and she didn't want to try to "escape from her problems in religion."

The counselor agreed with everything Natalie said and

asked for permission to share the one and only reason that Natalie should ever consider a relationship with the Lord. Natalie agreed with an attitude of "what have I got to lose?" – and the counselor shared the plan of salvation with her, assuring her that the only reason to trust Christ was if she recognized that she was a sinner who knew that she could not save herself, but accepted the gift of eternal life through Jesus' death on the cross – the sacrifice for her sin.

Natalie was quiet for several moments, then she sat up straighter in her chair. "I have been thinking about this for two weeks. I believe that the reason God has brought me here today was so you could tell me about the reason – the only reason – that I should give my life to Christ. I don't think it is an accident that your scheduled client didn't show up…that allowed you to fit me in. I'm ready to ask Jesus to save me."

They prayed together, and Natalie prayed a sweet prayer, asking Jesus to forgive her sin. She thanked Him for dying for her so that she could have eternal life. She received Him with gladness.

The pregnancy test was negative and Natalie and the counselor both breathed a sigh of relief. The counselor shared from God's word about the issue of sex and singleness. Natalie admitted that she needed to change her thinking in that area. She asked the counselor to pray for her.

At the end of the session, the counselor asked, "May I have your permission to give you a hug?" Before the words were fully out of her mouth, Natalie had almost leapt into her arms and hugged right back!

"Oh, yes! Thank you for being honest with me and not trying to force Jesus into my life. Thank you, thank you!"

Hope Pregnancy Centers
Broward County, Florida

A Different Kind of Prayer

This prayer is based on an Internet Article that was making its rounds a couple of years ago. I adapted it for the pregnancy care center ministry and gave it to our center directors and volunteers. I have tried to find out who authored the original "prayer", but to no avail. I submit my adaptation to be dedicated to all of the faithful servants who are out there on the frontlines of the battle for life – giving full credit to whoever wrote the original words that inspired this!

Heavenly Father,

Help us remember that the jerk who cut us off in traffic last night might be a **single, pregnant mother** who worked nine hours yesterday and was rushing home to cook dinner, help her eight-year-old with homework, do the laundry and spend a few precious moments with her child before bedtime.

Help us to remember that the pierced, tattooed, disinterested young man at the grocery store check-out counter is a worried nineteen-year-old college student who may have just gotten the news that **his girlfriend is pregnant**. The apprehension over final exams pales in comparison to the news of his impending fatherhood.

Give us grace, Lord, when we lose patience with the rowdy group of teenagers in the mall, and help us remember that they are struggling with decisions about their sexual behavior and are under tremendous pressure from a society that says "everybody's doing it." Many of them are already **grieving for the purity they have given away**.

Remind us, Lord, that the scary looking bum who begs for money on the street corner became a slave to addictions (that we can only imagine in our worst nightmares) because he needed something to **dull the pain of the abortion** he pressured his girlfriend to have when they were in college.

Help us to be patient with the older couple who walks slowly through the mall; they may be **grieving the loss of the grandchild** that they have just learned was lost to abortion.

Heavenly Father, remind us each day that, of all the gifts you give us, **the greatest gift is life.** It is not enough to celebrate life only with those we hold dear. **Open our eyes** to all of the types of suffering that accompany unplanned pregnancies. **Open our eyes** to the fact that these issues affect all our families…not just our blood families, but our church families, and the family of humanity all around us, as well. **Let us be slow to judge and quick to forgive; quick to show patience, empathy and love.**

All of us are affected by abortion…whether we know it or not.

~Amen
Nancy McDonald
Hope Pregnancy Centers
Broward County, Florida

YOUR CHILD MAY BE MENTALLY OR PHYSICALLY CHALLENGED

Jonathan son of Saul had a son who was lame in both feet. He was five years old when...his nurse picked him up and fled, but as she hurried to leave, he fell and became crippled. His name was Mephibosheth.
II Samuel 4:4

Don't be afraid, David said to him, for I will surely show you kindness for the sake of your father Jonathan. I will restore all the land that belonged to your grandfather Saul, and you will always eat at my table.
II Samuel 9:7 NIV

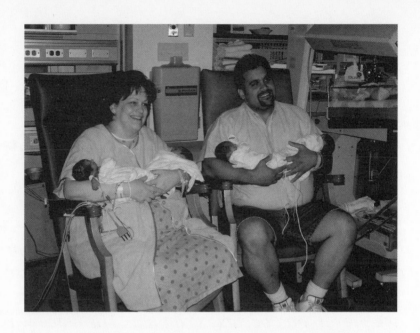

ARMS FILLED WITH BABIES

"Now to him who is able to do immeasurably more than all we ask or imagine, according to his power that is at work within us."
                                                            Ephesians 3:20

It had always been Stephen and LeAnn Beloyan's desire to have children. They were thrilled when LeAnn became pregnant about twelve years ago. They were devastated when their daughter, Rebecca LeAnn, was stillborn.

For about a year after this, they tried to get pregnant again. They went to a fertility doctor, but nothing happened. "We stopped because we just were not comfortable with the process," Stephen said.

After about ten years, they both felt God was telling them to try again. They went back to a fertility doctor and they got pregnant.

The second ultrasound they did showed one heartbeat. It appeared as a blinking dot. As the doctor continued to check LeAnn, he saw another sac; but there was nothing in it. He told them it looked like an embryo had started to grow, but stopped. He explained to them that this sometimes happened. "You could have twins, but I doubt it," were his infamous words.

The next week they went back for another ultrasound. As the doctor looked at it, he said, "Oh, you're going to have identical twins." He showed them the two dots indicating two heartbeats. Then he checked the other sac. "Oh, you're going to have triplets! The other embryo continued to grow." He then showed them the other heart beat.

About this time LeAnn asked him, "Are you sure, that's it? We are not going to come back next week and find more?"

The doctor said, "Well, let me look again." He began to look. Then he said, "Uh, oh!" Stephen became very scared and asked, "Is everything Okay?" The doctor kept looking, and then he said, "I've *never* seen this before!" These were two phrases you *never* want to hear your doctor say, and he had said them both."

With a look of amazement on his face, the doctor turned to them and said, "The two embryos have each split. You're going to have two sets of identical twins!"

"In a matter of minutes, we had gone from knowing we were going to have one baby, to twins, to triplets then to this – quadruplets!"

Having two sets of identical twins is so rare that the doctors weren't even sure of the odds. The CDC (Center for Disease Control) statistics estimate that the odds of giving birth to quadruplets are about 1 in 1,000,000 quadruplet births. But having two sets of identical twins places the odds much higher. Some say these odds are estimated to be 1 in 1 million to 1 in 25 million. *That's rare indeed*!

After they found out they were pregnant with four babies, the doctors were concerned about the multiple births because of

171

the difficulties that could occur during pregnancy; there were risks for the mother as well as the babies. Would she be able to carry the babies long enough for them to survive?

"The doctor who had helped us become pregnant did not bring up reduction, (aborting two of the babies) because we had already explained our feelings to him. He knew under no circumstances would we abort any of the babies. But one or two of the doctors did bring it up. When we shared our feelings with them, they did not again try to talk us into reducing.

This in itself was an answer to prayer. We had prayed that we would not be harassed about aborting any of our babies."

The Beloyans' feeling was that the God who had created the universe was the God who had created their babies, and He was perfectly able to care for ALL of them !

LeAnn shared, "Several years ago I went to some of the real prayer warriors in our church and asked them to pray specifically that God would give us twins. I was asking them to pray for this as having twins *was* the desire of our hearts. They had prayed this for years. *God just chose to double our request!* I wouldn't change it for anything!"

She continued, "Seven years ago a childhood friend of mine promised God that she would give up chocolate (This was a real sacrifice for her; as she was a real chocoholic!) if He would *not just give us a child*, but would fill our arms with children. She was getting antsy. She asked, 'OK, God what's going on? Are you going to do it?'

Shortly after she asked God this question, we were able to share with our church about our pregnancy. This is when my friend told me of her promise to God. I did not know this until this time. God truly had answered her prayers. He had given each of us a child for each of our arms!"

The answers to specific prayers for this couple were amazing. The doctors had told LeAnn she would almost certainly become a diabetic during her pregnancy; she never became a diabetic. They told her her blood pressure would go up; it didn't. They told her she would get pre-ecclampsia; she didn't (until after the babies were born). They warned her that she might go into pre-term labor; she didn't.

We would later learn that unknown to us, different people were praying for *each* of these specific things.

LeAnn said, "I was fearful of the pregnancy. I was thirty-six years old, and I was a high risk especially for multiple births. I had three strikes against me, my age, past history, and a multiple pregnancy. But as I began to hear how people were praying for specific things and seeing how God was already answering these prayers, I felt a real peace. All in all, it was a wonderful pregnancy. I never got sick; no problems other than the eight week stay in the hospital."

All along the doctors had told them thirty-two weeks was the perfection number for quads. Most quads are born at twenty-nine weeks. At twenty-five weeks LeAnn was admitted to the hospital. Her cervix was starting to open. "We thought we were coming in early, but the doctors told us they expected us a week ago." At thirty-one weeks the doctors looked at the ultrasound and said they felt like they should take the babies the following week (week 32 – perfection week!).

"They gave us a choice of having the babies on a Tuesday or a Wednesday. Since LeAnn was ready for them to come, we chose Tuesday. The doctors wanted their births scheduled so they would have enough help in the delivery room. There would be a total of twenty-one people there to assist. If it were an emergency delivery, they would not have as many people available to assist."

The delivery went exceptionally well. Lauren Leigh and her identical twin, Sarah Grace, were born first; followed by Benjamin Stephen and Samuel Matthew. They were all delivered within about four minutes.

"That night after the births, LeAnn showed signs of pre-ecclampsia (high blood pressure, fluid retention). The people's

173

prayers had been that she get none of these while she was pregnant. She DIDN'T! If she had gotten pre-ecclampsia before the babies were born, there would have been a much greater risk for both her and the babies. The doctors told us they would have had to take the babies on Tuesday with LeAnn's health conditions changing; so things would have been much worse if Wednesday rather than Tuesday had been chosen as the delivery day.

She had to take magnesium for the pre-ecclampsia. This has many side affects that we were concerned about. I called one of our friends and asked her to pray for LeAnn, that she have no side affects. She prayed at that moment and assured me she would pray for LeAnn all night.

LeAnn had NO side affects from the medication."

When asked by the media what they wanted for their babies, Stephen's reply was, "I want them to come to know the Lord at an early age and to follow Him!"

What more could any parent wish for their children?

Jeanetta Bearden Pollard

174

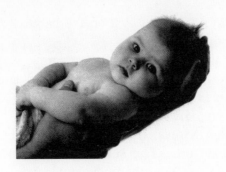

WE GIVE THANKS

They named her Angel. The father held her in his arms and gave thanks, saying, *"This baby has made our family complete."* During one Thanksgiving season, there was a family in Broward County who was very thankful for the gift that God gave them, wrapped up in a sweet baby girl. But that's the **end** of the story... let's go back a few months, before that Thanksgiving, and I'll tell you about the day we met Angel's mother.

She came in for the free pregnancy test, fearful that, at the age of forty-two, she might be pregnant again. She had one twenty-year old daughter and an eight-year old. Her plan for her future did not include a baby. She told the counselor she would abort right away if the test were positive.

The test was positive and the counselor gently shared these words from Jeremiah 1:5: *"I knew you before I formed you in your mother's womb and set you apart."* Tears of sorrow coursed down the woman's face as the realization dawned on her that she was considering ending the life of a baby that God had sent her as a special gift. Sorrow turned to joy as she made a decision to carry the baby and face the future with a hope that God would provide. She left that day thanking God that He had led her to Hope Pregnancy Centers.

A few months later, we received the shocking news that a

routine sonogram revealed a cyst on the baby's brain and that an abortion was being scheduled.

In faith, this family asked us to pray; they went to their church and asked for more prayer. They fasted, and they asked for God's miraculous intervention and healing. They totally yielded to His sovereignty and His plan.

The mother requested another sonogram before she would submit to the abortion. **The sonogram was completely clear!** What praising and rejoicing there was in Heaven and on earth that day! Angel's mother told her counselor, *"God dried my tears and gave me a peace that everything was going to be all right."* Her sense of peace became reality when she delivered a perfect baby girl a few weeks later!

Hope Pregnancy Centers
Broward County, Florida

MOTHER'S DAY

This month we celebrate Mother's Day. In this letter, we would like to pay tribute to one special mother who met Jesus face to face on Saturday, May 2, 2003. Her name was Sandra. She was one of our first clients. She had stayed in touch with us over the years. She and her daughter, Gabrielle, have a very special place in our hearts.

In a very bizarre and difficult situation, she chose life for her baby. Gabrielle and Sandy were a very integral part of our beginnings. We mourn the untimely death of this young woman.

She was one of the very first clients who came to us when we opened our doors in 1991. The method of birth control she had chosen was Norplant, which was advertised to be "foolproof."

She had gone to the doctor at the university's medical clinic when she suspected that she was pregnant. "Impossible!" was the doctor's response to her fears. As the weeks passed, not only did they recognize the reality of her pregnancy – they put heavy pressure on her to abort. First they told her that the baby would not grow. They were wrong. Then they told her the baby would be severely damaged by the heavy dosages of hormones from the Norplant. They were wrong. She trusted God at every turn, and got support from her counselor at Hope. She was ready to face whatever God brought her way.

In a final attempt to coerce her to terminate the pregnancy, they offered her $10,000 to have an abortion so that the "fetus" could be studied – almost making it sound like a noble sacrifice for the cause of science. Sandra stood her ground and God proved his faithfulness.

Gabrielle was born healthy and beautiful. She did everything early or on time, according to the baby books, and God even threw in a little voice that could sing like an angel! One year banquet guests enjoyed a blessing in song from this little child

177

whose life was spared. Our volunteers have been blessed by having Gabrielle come to some of our meetings and sing for us, too. Sandra stayed in touch with us over the years. We knew she was madly in love with this little girl.

Towards the end of April, Sandra called, and I spoke with her on the phone. She was so proud of her daughter! Gabrielle is a young lady now, getting ready for middle school. Sandra wanted to be a good mom; so she was calling to set up an appointment to talk with our abstinence director to learn how to teach abstinence and purity to her daughter. During that conversation, we made plans for Gabrielle to sing at an upcoming event. The day before I received the tragic news of Sandra's death, I got the response card in the mail for the tea party that I had invited them to. It is hard to imagine that I will not hear Sandra's voice or see her face again this side of Heaven.

Brave young women like Sandra are making decisions at Hope everyday in order to save the lives of babies like Gabrielle! As a ministry, and as individuals, we are richer for having known Sandra. We remember her with gladness, and we will miss her. Celebrate life today... Sandra's death is a reminder that today is the only day we truly have.

Hope Pregnancy Centers
Broward County, Florida

DOUBLE THE LOVE

Hi, my name is Stephanie, and I know that you are the parents God has chosen for my babies," a young woman said over the phone to Tyler and Mark Rosenquist.
"Did you say *babies*?" Tyler asked.

After losing three babies to miscarriage, the Rosenquists began to pursue adoption. They had gone through medical tests and suffered the heartache that only childless couples understand. So a call like this left Tyler tongue-tied, excited and nervous.

"How anxious I was, talking to a woman who could answer all my dreams." Tyler says.

Although the Rosenquists weren't listed for twins on the adoption profile, when Stephanie read their paperwork, she knew this was the family her children needed.

Two Mothers

As an 18-year-old, Stephanie had been dating an abusive boyfriend for two years. In desperation one day, she asked God to remove him from her life. Four days later, the boyfriend was arrested for drunk driving in a hit-and-run accident, and as a result of his actions was sentenced to serve time in jail.

But a few weeks after the arrest, Stephanie found out she was pregnant. Confused and scared, Stephanie considered abortion. Then she talked with a youth pastor who helped her understand that abortion was not the answer. Shortly after that, an ultrasound confirmed she was having twins! Not only was she pregnant, unwed and scared, but now she had two little lives to think about, too.

Stephanie gave her life to Christ and instead of thinking about herself, she asked God what was best for her babies. "God gave me peace about adoption. and I fell in love with the possibility of placing my babies," Stephanie says. Soon after that, she connected with ChristianAdoption.com and called the Rosenquists.

"We were friends from that first phone call on," Tyler says. After the Rosenquists discussed Stephanie's request, they accepted the offer and made plans to be Mom and Dad to twins.

Two Babies

A month later, blood tests showed a problem, and an ultrasound confirmed that one of the babies had spina bifida (an opening in the back that exposes the spine) and probably hydrocephalus (fluid on the brain). Doctors advised Stephanie to have a selective abortion, but she refused.

"[The prognosis] is as mild as it can be," Stephanie told Tyler in tears. "He may be in diapers and have to wear leg braces the rest of his life. They're most worried about the hydrocephalus, because it causes brain damage."

"It was the most devastating news I'd ever received," Tyler admits. "I had dreams, and when I found out my child may never walk, may be mentally retarded, I thought, *What shallow dreams!*"

But Tyler and Mark were already parents in their hearts. "At that moment, we named him Andy," Tyler says. "He was my child, and I didn't care if he was picture perfect. He's exactly the way God created him."

Both families planned and worked together for the good of the boys. When the babies were born, Matthew was perfectly normal.

Then Andy was born, and his condition was worse than expected. Along with spina bifida and hydrocephalus, Andy's hips were displaced, his feet were clubbed, and he had a half-pound growth on this back.

The following day, doctors operated on Andy to remove the growth and close up his spine. A few days later, they removed fluid from his brain but suspected he suffered from brain damage.

Three and a half years later, Andy has amazed the doctors by walking, even running, and developing normally. "He is the epitome of a strong-willed child. God has given him the gift to overcome obstacles," Tyler says. "And Matthew has been an inspiration to him. Because Matt does everything first, Andy wants to keep up." And although Andy still wears diapers and probably always will, he's healthy.

Matthew and Andy are double blessings to two families. Stephanie visits occasionally, and the boys love her dearly. Challenges, hope and unselfish love for two little boys - God's sweet plan for them all.

Susan Graham Mathis

In reference to the Roe v. Wade decision that was handed down on January 25, 1973, in her book

"Sitting By My Laughing Fire Side"

Ruth Bell Graham, the author says:

"Of this day, two things I kept:
The earth was cold and grey and heaven wept."

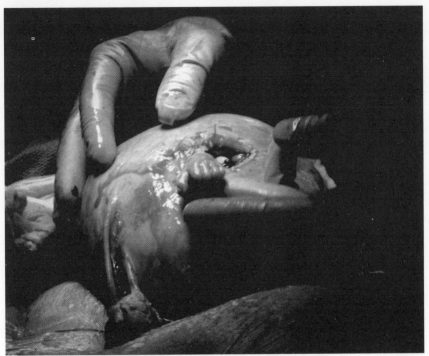

BABY SAMUEL'S STORY

"Samuel Armas made more of an impact on this world before he was born than most of us make in a lifetime."

Michael Clancy

The photo is perhaps the most amazing of the Twentieth Century. Take a look near the center of the photo and you will see the tiny hand of a 21-week-old fetus as it appears through a tiny slit in the womb.

"As a doctor asked me what speed of film I was using, out of the corner of my eye I saw the uterus shake, but no one's hands were near it. It was shaking from within. Suddenly, an entire arm thrust out of the opening, then pulled back until just a little hand was showing. The doctor reached over and lifted the hand, which reacted and squeezed the doctor's finger. As if testing for strength, the doctor shook the tiny fist. Samuel held firm. I took the picture! Wow!"

Michael Clancy who had been hired by USA Today to photograph the surgery said this had made a pro-lifer out of him.

Samuel's parents learned before their son was born that he had spina bifida, a hole in his spine that could leave him physically and mentally disabled. Although they were literally torn apart by the news, aborting the baby was not an option for Julie and Alex Armas. They had always believed that life begins at conception. Their feeling was that they had wanted a child and this was the one God had chosen to give them.

One of the reasons Julie and Alex decided to give USA Today an interview was because of the fact that it is believed that the majority of babies with spina bifida are aborted in this country (at least one half). They wanted people to know that there was an educated, professional couple who love and value their child even though he is "defective" by the world's definition.

One of the main reasons the Armas decided to do the surgery was the hope that the prevention of one of the most devastating complications of spina bifida - retardation might be prevented. They weren't concerned about a child who couldn't walk, but they wanted a child who would know them.

This could be a miraculous intervention to prevent further damage or, as Dr. Bruner told Julie, a very expensive miscarriage. The operation should take about an hour, but it would seem like a life time to the family waiting.

The instruments were designed to work in miniature. They would be working on a fetus that could fit in the palm of your hand. The sutures that would close the incisions were less than the thickness of a human hair, almost invisible.

At one point during the operation, the surgeon whispered,

184

"Shh! You'll wake the baby."

As the uterus was placed back in the abdomen, someone exclaimed, "Beautiful," and the tenseness in the room gave way to a sigh of relief. Mother and child were doing well - they had survived the surgery.

Samuel's mother was quoted as saying she and her husband "wept for days" when they saw the photo. The photo reminded them [that] the pregnancy wasn't about disability or illness. It was about a little person.

When asked about her son, his mother said that he was the cutest thing you have ever seen.

"On Samuel's first Thanksgiving, as I was making breakfast my heart and tears started overflowing with praise to God for his goodness in general, but especially where my precious angel was concerned. Most of all, I am thankful to Him for allowing me to be born into a home where I was given the Christian heritage and values that would not allow me to make a 'choice' that would have denied me the sheer joy of knowing this child..."

When Samuel was nearly four-years-old, he along with his parents testified before a US Senate Subcommittee about the experience with utero surgery. They were joined by Dr. James Thorp, a maternal-fetal medicine specialist, and by Michael Clancy, the photographer who captured Samuel's awe-inspiring grip.

Alex spoke of his son. He is nearly four-years-old and has not had to endure the surgeries that are common to most children with spina bifida. He walks with leg braces and is cognitively normal. He loves to catch bugs.

According to doctors, the average child with spina bifida who has surgery after birth will spend more than six months in the hospital and endure more than six major operations in the first five years of his life.

When Samuel was shown a large-scale version of his in

185

utero photograph and asked if he knew what it was, his reply was, "Baby Samuel."   When asked what the doctors did to him that day, he replied, "They fixed my boo-boo."

Samuel's father said he and his wife never considered such a terrible diagnosis could lead to "blessings."

POST ABORTION

"As far as the east is from the west,
So far has he removed
Our transgressions from us."

~Psalms 103:12 NIV~

SISTERS IN CHRIST

Sisters in Christ are we,
Sharing something so personal and deep.
Each with a story to tell,
That was hidden deep inside a well.
Brought together in love
Handpicked by the Lord above.
He healed our wounds with His words,
And gave us forgiving grace that was undeserved.
The things that we learned we will never forget,
God was a comfort in a time of regret.
That warm safe place where we confided,
Jehovah-Jireh was the one that provided.
Departing from one another
Vowing always to love the other.
Sisters in Christ are we,
Sharing something so personal and deep.

~ Bev '93

Hope Pregnancy Centers
Broward County, Florida

Melody Rose

Delightful news danced in my heart as I practically skipped up the sidewalk to my house. I was pregnant with our third child! Wonderful news! The excitement was greater than my fear that my husband may not welcome another child. I burst through the front door and blurted out my news, eager to see his response.

In a single moment, my joy turned to anguish. My husband threatened to leave me if I gave birth to this baby. "You can get an abortion," he said, "or you'll have three kids to raise by yourself. You decide."

I was shocked. I was devastated that he could so callously tell me to abort our child. I was pushed into a dark prison where sorrow and confusion were my cellmates. Lose my husband – the father of my two growing children? Lose a baby I hadn't met? It was an impossible and unfair choice. My heart ached with the weight of the decision. Do I follow my husband's wishes? Do I have a baby that he doesn't want and risk his walking out on my children and me?

Abandonment took on a new meaning for me. I retreated into a world of "what if" thinking. I felt incapable of standing up to his threats. There was no one I could talk to. If I told my Christian parents what he was suggesting, they would be appalled. I knew that I would never tell them if I chose to have the abortion. Satan uses secrecy as a weapon against us – and he certainly kept me from going to godly people who could have given me wise counsel to help me make a right choice.

I thought about talking to someone at the small church I was attending, but again, I couldn't even fathom talking to Christians about aborting my baby – or admitting that my husband was pressuring me to do such a horrific thing. My own sense of inferiority kept me from reaching out – I would pick up the phone to call the pastor or a church member – but the fear of condemnation always caused me to hang up quickly before anyone answered. I also lived with the fear of my husband's anger if he found out I had talked to anyone about such a personal matter. I had experienced his jealous rages in the past over much less important matters.

I told myself I just needed to get some facts. My mother was a nurse, and I had access to her medical books. I looked for answers about when a fetus became a baby. I couldn't seem to find a clear answer – and because I didn't have a car, it never occurred to me that a library might have more information. Nothing was clear to me – now I know that one of Satan's trademarks is confusion. I was utterly confused.

I'm not sure if I prayed or not – I just had this overwhelming feeling that I had to figure everything out for myself and by myself. I had strayed very far from the God of my childhood – I was now idolizing my spouse who did not know God.

As the clocked ticked and the days dragged on, I began to feel I had no choice. I lived with the daily threat that he would leave me. My heart ached as I looked at my two little boys, ages two and four...I would deprive them of a brother or sister or I would deprive them of their father. How would I feed them and clothe them if their father left me? Who would care for them if I had to go to work? I loved their father. I did not want the disgrace and heartache of divorce to touch my little family. I decided to terminate my pregnancy. I had no idea of the life of grief and sorrow that lay ahead of me.

Members of my husband's family arrived as the day for the "procedure" drew near. They would help with the children during my "hospitalization". I wanted to talk to his sister and plead my case for giving life to my baby. But I couldn't even talk about it. I assumed she would support my husband, so I didn't discuss it with her at all. My husband made all the arrangements at our local hospital, so it would be "safe." As we drove to the hospital I

190

wanted to scream, "Stop the car! I can't go through with this!"
Didn't he see my face? Didn't he know my heart was breaking?

My family waited in the lobby and drank coffee and read
magazines while I was taken to the fifth floor. A large kindly man
told me to take off my clothes and put on the hospital gown.
Random thoughts floated in and out of my head. I wondered what
my jealous husband would say if he knew this man stood there and
watched me undress. I remember feeling so violated and helpless
and vulnerable.

I wondered what would happen if I just told this doctor
that I didn't want to end my baby's life. I wanted someone to
know my pain – I wanted someone to provide a way out for me
and for my baby...but crazy thoughts kept invading my mind:
"This man works here – he's not going to tell me not to do
this...and besides, my husband is waiting downstairs... if I don't
do this, he will beat me up."

I felt lost and totally unable to control what was happening
to me. I hated myself for allowing it to proceed. I screamed
inside, but no one heard my cries. They put me on a stretcher and
parked me in a long line of stretchers, all filled with other women
waiting for their "simple, safe procedures."

A nurse rushed by me, carrying a bowl that appeared to be
filled with blood and tissue. I kept repeating "I can't do this", but
no one seemed to be listening. They gave me an injection to calm
me down. When I tried to yell, the words would not come. I tried
to get off the stretcher, but I could not move.

When I woke up in the recovery room, I muttered "Thank
God it's over" again and again. I wanted attention from the nurses
– but they were all business and gave me no extra care. I
remember thinking, "this horrible nightmare is over and now life
can get back to normal." I was so wrong. My life has never been
the same as it was before the abortion.

That night and every night for months and months, I cried
myself to sleep. My husband never asked how I felt or why I

191

cried. He slept through my tears. But my desire for him and my love for him died completely. How could he want to kill our baby? How could he say he loved me and let me suffer this tragic loss? I distanced myself from him and withdrew into an angry hardened shell. Two years later we were divorced. How ironic that the marriage I had sacrificed my baby for was doomed to fail anyway!

Several years passed and God began to call me back to Himself. He rescued me from the downward spiral of the years following the abortion. I had drifted into a lifestyle of immorality to drown my sense of worthlessness and depression. Guilt and shame consumed me and I could not stop crying every time I thought about the abortion. I tortured myself with thoughts of how old my child would be; I would see children in the mall and envy the mothers who had chosen life. I missed my baby every single day.

I saw a therapist once a week for nearly eighteen years after my abortion. He encouraged me to put the past behind me and move on with my life. As I matured in my Christian walk, I stopped seeing this secular therapist and turned to a Christian psychologist for help. She believed the abortion was the root of my depression and asked me if I had ever heard of a Bible Study called "Forgiven and Set Free".

Feeling little hope that God could forgive me, I reluctantly followed her advice and contacted the local ministry that offered this Bible Study. I knew it was time to put the abortion behind me, but I also knew that it was something I could not do on my own.

The tremendous peace and understanding that I experienced in each one of the twelve sessions of the Bible Study gave me comfort and assurance. I began to really believe that God's forgiveness, grace, and mercy were gifts that He meant for me to experience!

A new hope was born in my heart as I came week after week. Other women were looking for healing and forgiveness, too. They understood my pain – they had lived it, too. The two women who led the class had also experienced the pain of abortion in their own lives. Their prayers and God's intervention allowed me to experience true restoration.

The abortion was thirty years ago. The healing continues, even today, as I write this testimony. Satan laid a trap that he meant to use to ensnare me for a lifetime, but God has rescued me. He confirmed to me through the Bible Study what I had always felt in my heart: I have a daughter to hold when I get to Heaven. Her name is Melody Rose and she is safe in Jesus' arms until I get there to take her into mine.

Since abortion was legalized in 1973, women have believed lies that have led to the slaughter of millions of innocent children…children like my own precious Melody Rose. Every day the Accuser tries to return me to the past to wallow in regrets and the what-ifs – but I remind him that IN CHRIST JESUS I AM A NEW CREATION! I don't deserve God's grace towards me, but I am SO THANKFUL that my sin is covered with the blood of Jesus and my slate is wiped clean.

~ Melody Rose's mom
Hope Pregnancy Centers
Broward County, Florida

"A day never goes by that I do not think of it"
"Since it happened, I have never told another living soul about it."

What is IT?

Abortion is the secret that we are talking about. Women and men who have experienced abortion often make the two statements quoted above. This story will give you a glimpse inside the important work of **Hope Restored,** a ministry for women and men who desire reconciliation with God.

ONE WOMAN'S STORY

"Years ago, in the midst of a crisis pregnancy, I reached for the only solution anyone offered to me. I chose abortion. THE 'problem' was solved, but MY problems were just beginning.

In the aftermath of the abortion, my life spiraled downward. I experienced an over-whelming sense of shame and failure that impacted every area of my life. I withdrew from family, friends and studies. I felt so changed by the abortion. I desperately wanted to change what I had done – who I had become. But there seemed no way back.

Depression characterized my life for years. But the mind can play strange tricks. After a while I barely remembered the abortion. In fact, I never discussed it or acknowledged it. I denied it to everyone, including myself. I blamed my sadness on the people around me and on my circumstances.

After becoming a Christian and getting involved in a local church, I heard about a place called Hope Pregnancy Centers. I decided to attend their volunteer training seminar. In the back of my mind I thought, "Maybe I can help young women in crisis pregnancies make a better choice than I made when I was in college." I certainly had NO intention of sharing my experience with anyone! It was during that training seminar that I heard a woman talk about her abortion experience. As she spoke, the wall of denial I had erected around my heart collapsed, and an ocean of grief was released.

This was the beginning of my healing and restoration. Through a Bible Study entitled "Forgiven and Set Free", administered by Hope Pregnancy Centers, I worked my way through acknowledging the truth about my abortion, grieving the loss of that child, and receiving God's forgiveness at a level that finally allowed me to forgive myself.

****

Hope Restored is the quiet portion of our ministry that is offered almost exclusively to the body of Christ. In a safe, extremely confidential environment, we offer a twelve-week Bible Study that leads participants to discover God's character. Once they understand His mercy and forgiveness, they are able to process the fact that even their abortion is forgiven by the Father. They walk away from this study, "Forgiven and Set Free." *There is Hope Restored because Jesus covered ALL of our sins at Calvary.*

Hope Pregnancy Centers
Broward County, Florida

POST ABORTION HEALING

"A.C." came to us offering to help us minister to women in unplanned pregnancies. She was one of those women who are easy to envy. To an observer, she had it all. She was married to a godly man; was a stay at home mom. She had two sweet kids and was a leader in her church and the community.

God has richly blessed us here at Hope. He sends his best to volunteer with us, so even though we were excited to have her at our training, we were not surprised that He would call her to minister alongside us. She came to give the gift of herself.

As is often the case, God had another plan. "A.C." thought she was coming here to give something to us. Instead, the Father gently called her to Hope so she could receive some gifts that He had prepared for her a long, long time ago.

Conservative estimates say that one in four members of evangelical churches are post-abortive. It is hard to get a true number because an abortion is one of the last things that any Christian man or woman wants to dredge up from the past and think about – much less talk about. Almost eighteen years of ministry here in Broward County have shown us that the local number is probably much higher that that.

196

Where does a Christian woman or man go to talk about the pain and regret of a past-abortion decision? Many of them come to Hope Pregnancy Centers. Like the client I am describing, they don't usually come asking for us to help them – they come offering to help us because they want to help people make better choices than they did.

During the course of the training, "A.C." discovered that there were some tender places in her spirit that she had not fully surrendered to the Lord. As one of our staff members shared her own abortion story, this beautiful volunteer trainee (who looked so totally together on the outside) realized that there were some unfinished places on the inside of her heart that needed healing and restoration. They were related to an abortion she had experienced in college.

The P.A.C.E. program (post-abortion counsel and education) was the vehicle that God used to put her firmly on the path where He wanted her. She told us that the phrase "alive in Christ" took on a whole new meaning in her life, as she finally understood the depth of His love and forgiveness. The twelve-week Bible study was manna to her soul, and she finished the course rejoicing in the fact that she was "forgiven and set free."

"A.C." continues to train to serve at Hope, knowing that God can use every experience in her life to bring glory to Himself. In her exit evaluation "A.C." wrote: "The burden of shame and guilt that I carried for so long is gone! I understand in a whole new way about the freedom that Christ can give."

The aftermath of abortion is a "pregnancy-related crisis." We must keep telling them the whole truth in every area of our ministry. *There is hope for healing and restoration following an abortion.*

Hope Pregnancy Centers
Broward County, Florida

THIS FAR THE LORD HAS BROUGHT ME

It's always best to start at the beginning.

The journey begins. I am carrying several packages. They are all wrapped differently. The only thing that they have in common is that they stick out in ways that don't allow me to get close to anyone. They especially interfere with me getting close to the Lord. They prohibit me from feeling His loving arms around me.

I received all of these packages the day that I decided to have an abortion.

The first package was the most innocuous. It was small and wrapped in common brown paper. There was nothing to draw attention to it. It was easy to hide. Inside the plain brown wrapper was my Doubt – my doubt in the Lord and my lack of faith in the mighty things He was capable of doing.

The second and third packages were small, too – but their weight was overwhelming. They were hard to carry, and with every step I tried to take forward, they seemed to grow heavier and heavier. Those packages were Guilt and Shame.

The fourth package was very large. It was brightly wrapped and stood out – even from a distance. Everyone I met could see it plainly. It wasn't that I *wanted* everyone to see it – I just couldn't hide it. Anger was ill concealed in the fourth package that I carried.

The journey of my life continued, and I became accustomed to the packages I carried. The fitness gurus tell us that endurance training is all about conditioning. I was conditioned to carry my packages everywhere I went. I told myself I was doing just fine.

One day, I came to a fork in the road. The road to the left looked familiar – just as the road I had been traveling on for years and years. The road to the right was rugged terrain – it looked like a difficult path to walk. There were visible obstacles and crooked

198

turns and curves and I could not see what dangers might lie ahead. I almost turned away and chose familiarity. But then I heard someone calling my name.

I listened carefully, thinking the voice sounded familiar. Could it be the Lord? Yes! It was His still, small voice urging me to take the difficult path. Why, Lord? Why on earth would you want me to walk that way – haven't I had a hard enough time on the level path with all these packages I have to carry? But the voice was persuasive, and His promises to walk with me were irresistible…so I walked on.

No sooner had I turned the first corner, than I came upon a huge boulder that completely blocked the path. There was no way to get past it. I sat down in dismay, feeling hopeless. But the voice whispered in my ear again. "Yes, Lord?" I answered. "What is it that you want me to do?" He instructed me to take out the little package in the plain brown wrapper. As I took it out, He said to me, "I will instruct you and teach you in the way you should go; I will counsel you and watch over you." [Psalm 32:8]

He showed me that I would never be able to get past this first obstacle if I held onto the Doubt. I had to believe that He could do anything, just as He promised over and over again in His Word. I had to replace Doubt with Belief – that meant believing in Him and His power to forgive me, heal me, and help me forgive myself. I placed the package on top of the boulder and watched in amazement as the large rock turned into a tiny stone. I stepped over the stone and continued down this new path.

As I rounded the next bend, I saw that the road would take me to the edge of a great ravine. The cliffs on either side were steep, and there was only one-way to cross over the ravine: a large log was stretched between the two cliffs and the perilous ravine yawned below.

I looked quickly over my shoulder and saw that the Lord was still with me. I held up my hands as if to ask Him, "Now what?" He pointed to the two small packages.

"Lay them down," He said. He knew that they were heavy. He had watched me carry them for so long. He knew I couldn't cross over the ravine safely and still carry them with me.

First I took out Guilt and laid it at His feet. He looked at me with gentle eyes and said, "draw near to Me with a sincere heart in full assurance of faith, having your heart sprinkled to cleanse your guilty conscience and having your body washed with pure water." [Hebrews 10:4] Then I placed my Shame on the side of the road. When He saw that I had laid it down, He assured me, "No one whose hope is in me will ever be put to shame." [Psalm 25:3]

I felt so free! So lightweight – I nearly skipped across the log! Knowing He was walking with me gave me great confidence, and I had no fear of crossing the ravine. I thanked Him for helping me lay down my Guilt and Shame.

It was growing dark…there were so many trees along the path and the forest seemed to be reaching out to grab me and pull me into its darkness. I was so afraid that I would get lost. "Lord, are you still there?" I cried. "I can't see you – it's so dark!" That calm voice called me again and reminded me that I was still carrying a burden with me. It was the big package, with the bright wrapping named Anger. "That package is keeping you in darkness, child," He told me. "You have to lay it down if you want to walk with me." He said, "If you claim to have fellowship with Me yet walk in the darkness, you lie and do not live by the truth. But if you walk in the light, as I am in the light, you have fellowship with Me and my blood purifies you from all sin." [I John 1:6-7] As I laid Anger down at the edge of the forest, I was suddenly engulfed in light and I could see the path ahead!

As I came out of the darkness of the forest into the light, I realized that the path had completely circled back to the very place I had started! "Why would you lead me in a circle Lord – why take me through the obstacles, just to bring me back to this starting place again?"

"Because I want you to remember how it felt to be weighted down with the burdens that you carried – and I want you to know how it feels to travel the path now that you are forgiven and set free. I want you to look back over your journey and always remember that it is I – your Lord and Savior – that has brought you this far. I am the One who will carry you the distance."

So, I continue the journey. I still come to difficult places. I still find myself picking up things I am not supposed to carry. But I remember that there is One who walks along the path with me. He has brought me this far, and He has promised to never leave me or forsake me.

~Amen

Hope Pregnancy Centers
Broward County, Florida

PARENTAL NOTIFICATION

The following story has nothing to do with what pregnancy care centers do inside their offices. But it *does have* everything to do with our being involved in what is happening in our country. It *does have* to do with staying informed about laws; it *does have* to do with taking our values into the voting booth to exercise our privilege of voting for pro-life candidates. To us, these things, too, are important. We hope they are also important to you. This story could be about your daughter or granddaughter.

Testimony of Marcia Carroll concerning The Child Interstate Abortion Notification Act before the Subcommittee on the Constitution, U.S. House of Representatives March 3, 2005

My name is Marcia Carroll and the following is a horrifying series of events centered around my fourteen-year-old daughter.

On Christmas Eve 2004, my daughter informed me she was pregnant. My daughter chose to have the baby and raise it. My family fully supported my daughter's decision to keep her baby and we offered her our love and support.

Subsequently, her boyfriend's family began to harass my daughter and my family. They started showing up at our house to express their desire for my daughter to have an abortion. When that did not work, his grandmother started calling my daughter without my knowledge. They would tell her that if she kept the

203

baby, she couldn't see her boyfriend again. They threatened to move out of state. I told his family that my daughter had our full support in her decision to keep the baby. She also had the best doctors, counselors, and professionals to help her through the pregnancy. We all had her best interest in mind.

The behavior of the boy's family began to concern me to the point that I called my local police department for advice. Additionally, I called the number for an abortion center to see how old you have to be to have an abortion in our state.

I felt safe when they told me my minor daughter had to be sixteen years of age in the state of Pennsylvania to have an abortion without parental consent. I found out later that the Pennsylvania Abortion Control Act actually says that parental consent is needed for a minor under eighteen years of age. It never occurred to me that I would need to check the laws of other states around me. I thought as a resident of Pennsylvania that she was protected by Pennsylvania state laws, boy, was I ever wrong.

On February 16th, I sent my daughter to her bus stop with $2.00 of lunch money. I thought she was safe at school. She and her boyfriend had a prenatal class scheduled after school.

However, what really happened was that her boyfriend and his family met with her down the road from her bus stop and called a taxi. The adults put the children in the taxi to take them to the train station. His stepfather met the children at the train station, where he had purchased my daughter's ticket since she was only fourteen. They put the children on the train from Lancaster to Philadelphia. From there, they took two subways to New Jersey. That is where his family met the children and took them to the abortion clinic, where one of the adults had made the appointment.

When my daughter started to cry and have second thoughts, they told her they would leave her in New Jersey. They planned, paid for, coerced, harassed, and threatened her into having the abortion. They left her alone during the abortion and went to eat lunch.

204

After the abortion, his stepfather and grandmother drove my daughter home from New Jersey and dropped her off down the road from our house.

My daughter told me that on the way home she started to cry. They got angry at her and told her there was nothing to cry about.

Anything could have happened to my daughter at the abortion facility or on the ride back home. These people did not know my daughter's medical history, yet they took her across state lines to have a medical procedure without my knowledge or consent. Our family will be responsible for the medical and psychological consequences for my daughter as a result of this procedure that was completely unbeknownst to me.

I was so devastated that this could have been done that I called the local police department to see what could be done. They were just as shocked and surprised as I was that there was nothing that could be done in this horrible situation.

The state of Pennsylvania does have a parental consent law. Something has to be done to prevent this from happening to other families. This is just not acceptable to me and should not happen to families in this country. If your child goes to her school clinic for a headache, a registered nurse can't give her a Tylenol or aspirin without a parent's written permission.

As a consequence of my daughter being taken out of our state for an abortion without parental knowledge, she is suffering intense grief. My daughter cries herself to sleep at night and lives with this every day.

I think about what I could or should have done to keep her safe. Everybody tells me I did everything I could have and should have done. It doesn't make me feel any better, knowing everything I did was not enough to protect my daughter.

It does ease my mind to know with your help that we can make a difference and change the law to protect other girls and their families. I urge your support for *The Child Interstate*

Abortion Notification Act. It is critical that this law passes in Congress. The right of parents to protect the health and welfare of their minor daughters needs to be protected. No one should be able to circumvent state laws by performing an abortion in another state on a minor daughter without parental consent.

A MESSAGE FOR THOSE FIGHTING THE PRO-LIFE BATTLE

JUST PUSH

"Let us not grow weary in doing good, for at the proper time we will reap a harvest if we do not give up." ~ Galatians 6:9

A man was sleeping at night in his cabin when suddenly his room filled with light and God appeared. The Lord told the man he had work for him to do and showed him a large rock in front of his cabin. The Lord explained that the man was to push against the rock with all his might. So, this the man did, day after day.

For many years he toiled from sun up to sun down; his shoulders set squarely against the cold, massive surface of the unmoving rock, pushing with all his might. Each night the man returned to his cabin sore and worn out, feeling that his whole day had been spent in vain.

Since the man was showing discouragement, the Adversary decided to enter the picture by placing thoughts into the weary mind: "You have been pushing against that rock for a long time, and it hasn't moved," thus, giving the man the impression that the task was impossible and that he was a failure. These thoughts discouraged and disheartened the man. Satan said, "Why kill yourself over this? Just put in your time, giving just the minimum effort; and that will be good enough."

That's what he planned to do, but he decided to make it a matter of prayer and take his troubled thoughts to the Lord. "Lord," he said, "I have labored long and hard in your service, putting all my strength to do that which you have asked. Yet, after all this time, I have not even budged that rock by half a millimeter.

What is wrong? Am I a failure?"

The Lord responded compassionately, "My child, when I asked you to serve Me and you accepted, I told you that your task was to push against the rock with all your strength, which you have done. Never once did I mention to you that I expected you to move it. Your task was to push. And now you come to Me with your strength spent, thinking that you have failed. But is that really so? Look at yourself. Your arms are strong and muscled, your back sinewy and brown, your hands are calloused from constant pressure, your legs have become massive and hard. Through opposition you have grown much, and your abilities now surpass those which you used to have. Yes, you haven't moved the rock. But your calling was to be obedient and to push and to exercise your faith and trust in My wisdom. This you have done. Now I, my child, will move the rock."

Author Unknown

A Special Word To The Reader Of This Book

Now that you have read the book, perhaps you would like to know the One who is in the stories - the One who has helped individuals overcome whatever their problems were. We would like to help you find that One. He's always there waiting with open arms and willing to carry you through whatever crisis you are experiencing at this time. His name is Jesus and the Bible tells us in John 3:16 that He died so that you might live to have eternal life in Heaven.

John 3:16 says, "For God so loved the world that he gave his one and only Son, that whoever believes in him shall not perish but have eternal life."

In this verse the whoever is YOU! Now read the verse and put your name in the whoever blanks.

John 3:16: For God so loved _____ that

he gave his one and only Son, that if_____

believes in him_____

shall not perish but _____shall have eternal life."

Pray this simple, but powerful prayer so you can experience new life in Jesus.

Dear God, I thank you for sending Jesus to die for me. I ask you to forgive me for all of the things I have done wrong. Please come into my life and be my Savior. Lead me in the way You would have me to go. Thank you for hearing my prayer and giving me the assurance that I can know that I will live with you forever in Heaven.   Amen

Now that you have made this decision, please share it with someone.   You may contact us at 1-877-489-5645 or call one of the centers at 1-954-581-6992 or write to us at Success Ranch Publishers, PO Box 7, Boaz, Ky. 42027.   We would love to hear from you.   May God richly bless you is our prayer.

To locate a Pregnancy Care Center near you

Call 1-800-365-HELP

A *Member of*

To locate Hope Pregnancy Center, Inc.
In Broward County, Florida call 1-954-581-6992

212

A WORD FROM THE PUBLISHERS

Success Ranch Publishers is always interested in hearing from its readers. We are interested in your comments about our books.

We would also love to see any stories you would like to share with us. If you have any stories related to any of our books - stories related to anything having to do with unplanned pregnancies, abstinence, etc.; Christmas stories, please send them to us.

If you have an inspirational story, we always want to hear what God is doing in peoples' lives. You may contact us at:

Success Ranch Publishers
P.O. Box 7
Boaz, Kentucky 42027

You may email us at jim@successranch.com or visit our website at www.successranch.com or call us at 1-270-851-7699.

COMING FALL OF 2005
Santa's Little Instruction Book for Kids
by Jim Pollard

Cute instructions for life with illustrations for Kids of all ages. Following these instructions from Santa will make children's lives happier. It will also make for a better school and family life.

$9.95 plus $3.00 S&H*

To order send check or money order to:
Success Ranch Publishers, Inc.
P.O. Box 7
Boaz, Kentucky42027-0007
Or call 1-877-489-5645

*For orders of $24.00 or more, shipping is free.